THE JUNGLE

THE JUNGLE

A PERSONAL JOURNEY WITH THE ENFANT TERRIBLE OF NIGERIAN JOURNALISM

DAVID HUNDEYIN

Abibiman
Publishing

New York & London

First published in Great Britain in 2023
by Abibiman Publishing
www.abibimanpublishing.com

Copyright © 2023 by David Hundeyin

All rights reserved.
Published in the United Kingdom by
Abibiman Publishing,
an imprint of Abibiman Music & Publishing, London.

Abibiman Publishing is registered under
Hudics LLC in the United States and in the United Kingdom.

ISBN: 978-1-7392675-9-9

Cover Art by Frank Achulike
Cover design by Stephen Embleton

Printed in the United Kingdom by Clays Ltd.

Dedicated to the memories of my dad David Fakunle Hundeyin, my friend, colleague and 'big sister' Binta Bhadmus, and Iniobong Umoren, a lady whom I never met, but whose story is told in this book. I also wish to dedicate this book to my "nephew" Paul Armani Kato and my little Rwandan "niece" Keza Olubunmi. I hope you two will grow up to be as great as your moms are.

CONTENTS

I

THE UNTOLD STORY OF THE AEPB, ABUJA'S UNIFORMED FEMALE HARASSMENT UNIT

"They brought out two girls from the van and asked for money, those that didn't have money were all raped by the police, anyone that paid was allowed to go and from the van, if you had no money you'd be raped before they left you go off the van."

When Cynthia (name has been changed) went out with a group of her friends in Abuja on April 26, 2019, she probably envisaged a nice Friday night out with the girls after a hard week at work. Like many other single women living in Abuja, Cynthia was attracted to the relatively dynamic economy and vibrant, cosmopolitan lifestyle available in the federal capital. Unlike many other places in Nigeria where simply coming out at night is an extreme sport, the seat of Nigeria's federal government offered a semblance of normalcy.

The group of friends settled for a club called 'Cloud 9' at the Nadrem Emporium on 3rd Avenue, Gwarimpa. Suddenly the party was broken up by a large group of men who barged in, demanding that Cynthia and her friends stand up and follow them outside immediately. When they naturally resisted this unwanted intrusion on their evening outing, they were dragged outside along with the other women in the club. Outside they saw a convoy of law enforcement and armed forces vehicles including police, NSCDC, army, immigration and even the prisons service.

Cynthia didn't know it yet, but this would be the start of a 4-day ordeal in the hands of the police at the behest of the Abuja Environmental Protection Board (AEPB), a hitherto little-known agency which has since gained a fearsome reputation in the city, for its singular commitment to rape, extortion and harassment of young women. Over the ensuing 96 hours, she and at least 70 other young female detainees were tear-gassed in a locked police cell, denied food, water or sanitary provisions and raped by police officers if they could not pay for their freedom.

Their crime?

Apparently existing while female in Abuja.

Abuja's Targeted Female Raids: Officially Sanctioned Rape and Extortion Racketeering

While putting this story together, I spoke to six different victims of these raids, all of whom came from markedly different backgrounds and circumstances. While Cynthia was hanging out with her friends: Patricia, Mary and Judith at a club (all names have been changed), Mercy was standing at the roadside waiting for a "keke" while Peace was at a hotel for a friend's birthday. None of these women was doing anything particularly out of the ordinary, much less wrong. Yet, they all had more or less the same story, give or take a few details.

Mercy was accosted while waiting for a keke and abducted by a group of touts working for the AEPB. From going about her normal business, she found herself in police detention facing verbal and physical violence for no reason at all in the space of a few minutes. Even worse, as she said to my mounting amazement, she has been abducted under similar circumstances three times this year alone. For added incredulity, she revealed that on one such occasion, she was taken to the FCT High Court at Zuba and instructed to plead guilty to whatever she was charged with, otherwise, she risked going to Suleja prison.

My mouth nearly fell open when she said that she actually did so. Apparently, it really was a choice between pleading guilty to a nonsensical charge or finding herself remanded in a notorious prison in Niger State – for absolutely no reason. It did not escape my notice that this practice of scaring innocent people into pleading guilty to charges they do not understand could mean that a significant population of Suleja prison probably consists of innocent young women abducted from the streets of Abuja and forced to plead guilty to…anything including murder, terrorism and robbery.

Mercy got off fairly lightly, because she was charged only with "causing nuisance" – an offense which, while completely nonsensical, at least let her regain her freedom immediately. Peace on the other hand, was not so lucky. Of all the victims' horrible stories, hers perhaps was the most pitiful of the bunch because of how questionable it was. A regular middle-class professional working a 9-5 job, she was lodged in her hotel room celebrating a friend's birthday when she decided to buy water from the reception. Nobody answered the intercom, so she stepped out of her room to go downstairs herself. She did not even lock the door.

Describing what happened next she said:

> **"Immediately I got to the reception, one woman came and held my hands and insisted that I should follow her and I was like, "Ma, what happened?" She then said I should just respect myself**

and follow her, she continued dragging me until when we got outside, I saw cameras and a large crowd with people videoing with their phones, I saw so many hilux [sic] *with police, immigration civil defence, military, etc. They were just so many along with touts in reflective jackets. I saw other girls being dragged into the buses. They even went to the extent of knocking the hotel rooms, they will knock the hotel doors and if you open the door and you happen to be a lady, they will drag you out of the rooms into the buses, it got to one girl, they did not only drag her out of the hotel room, they dragged her and pull her clothes before the cameras and took a naked picture of her, they took her clothes off and she was naked and took pictures of her."*

Peace

The Curious Case of "Hajiya Safiya," Mastermind behind the Abduction of Abuja women

Through the course of the difficult conversations with all six women, one name kept coming up persistently as a chief protagonist of the newfangled rule-of-rape regime – a certain "Hajiya Safiya." A search on Google reveals some important things about this person. First of all, she appears to be a ghost. Despite currently being a high profile public servant in the nation's capital, Acting Secretary to the FCT Social Development Secretariat (SDS) Hajiya Safiya Umar, alias "Hajiya Safiya" has no pictures online, in the time honoured tradition of human rights luminaries like Col. Frank Omenka.

Second, Mrs. Umar appears to be something of a hypocrite. She is on record for criticizing Senator Elisha Abbo for assaulting a woman in July this year. Three months before that episode however, she directly and openly coordinated one of the worst human rights violations in the history of Nigerian democracy. Under her instruction, hundreds of women including nursing mothers were raped, assaulted, kidnapped and unlawfully detained in filthy conditions. She continues to defend her actions, while publicly condemning a woman-beater.

I mentioned that to properly contextualize the type of human being Mrs. Umar is; to all intents and purposes, she is one of those people.

Cynthia's description of her encounter with Hajiya Safiya revealed that while she was lucky enough to get out on Friday night, she came back on Saturday morning to bail out her friends, only to be thrown into the cell on the orders of this "Hajiya Safiya." Describing how it happened, she told me that upon getting to the station, she spotted a livid woman only known as "Hajiya Safiya," who wanted to know why the police granted bail to some of the girls from the previous night's raid. The lady did not want to know how the police did it, but she had one simple message for them:

"GET THOSE GIRLS BACK!"

Hajiya Safiya Umar

Due to the sheer misfortune of being present at the police station then, Cynthia was promptly rearrested, notwithstanding the N3, 000 she had already paid to bail herself out the previous night – a sum that was not refunded to her. Later that night, the police went out again on Hajiya Safiya's orders, abducting and detaining more women including a nursing mother with a two-month old baby.

When she appeared before the National Human Rights Commission on May 16 to explain the events of April 26, Mrs. Umar delivered the dismissive, nauseatingly self-righteous performance typical of Nigerian public office holders who think they are doing the country a favour by being in office. Responding to the well-established and widespread reports of rape and brutality that accompanied the Abuja raids, she flatly denied them and conveniently feigned ignorance of any such possibility. Presumably, it was a stretch to imagine that the famously professional and well-behaved lower ranks of the police could do such things when given free reign and assisted by civilian touts.

In between the gratuitous dishonesty though, she did freely admit to being one of the principal brains behind the April raids that launched the AEPB into its ferocious new phase of existence as a sort of female-focused SARS. In her view, these raids were necessary to tackle "social vices" like prostitution. In practice, that means carrying out the fool's errand of trying to group young women into "prostitutes" and "not prostitutes."

One might imagine that the Acting Secretary to the SDS – an institution that supposedly exists to help vulnerable women and children – would have a more nuanced and intelligent view of the world. Researching Hajiya Umar revealed however, that she has all the nuance and finesse of a chainsaw in a hardwood forest. To her, everything she considers a problem must be chopped down forthwith. Like prostitutes. Especially prostitutes. Actually only prostitutes. Also whoever she decides is a prostitute. Did I mention prostitute?

Prostitute.

According to her, the SDS and the AEPB collaboration was to preserve the "norms and values" of society, or at least the subjective ideas thereof held by she and her colleagues. In the face of several women who recounted their traumatising and dehumanising experiences, Mrs. Umar denied that any such thing could have happened, even though she also admitted that she had left the police station before the women were released – so she obviously had no way of confirming that.

> **"I was at Nadrem for a birthday and all of a sudden we saw some guys asking ladies to stand up and one guy walked up to me and insisted I should stand up, he said common will you stand up there, he then came and dragged me, inserting his hands in my buttocks in his attempts to drag me he was putting his hand in my ass and pressing my buttocks, and this was the hired touts they brought along to harass us."**
>
> *Patricia*

Meanwhile, as everyone struggles to identify precisely what "norms and values" Mrs. Umar and her syndicate are "preserving" in the federal capital by running an industrial harassment of women (with some repeatedly raped by Police) and extortion machine, it is very important to note that these raids were not a one-off event. They had been happening before April, albeit on a smaller scale, and they are still happening now, six months later. I may have addressed the stories of my six sources using the past tense, but the risk of abduction, sexual harassment, rape, torture and wrongful imprisonment is very much a present and ongoing risk for young women in Abuja.

Banana seller, office worker, shop owner, teenager, 30-something year-old, single, married – it doesn't really matter anymore. Young women in Nigeria's federal capital are now fair game for Safiya Umar and her motley crew of sexual perverts, rapists, sadists and dirty cops to do absolutely whatever they want to, with no consequences. Hajiya Safiya belongs to a school of binary thought that divides all young women into "prostitutes" and "not prostitutes." Apparently if you are a young woman in Abuja right now, who dares to breathe oxygen and exhibit bipedal motion, Hajiya Umar thinks you are a prostitute. And since you are a prostitute, you clearly deserve to be abducted, raped and extorted – maybe even killed.

The Unanswered Legal and Political Questions

Amid the outrage that surrounded the initial story of the AEPB raids earlier in the year, something that repeatedly kept coming up was the possibility that the AEPB was actually acting under the legal remit of what we euphemistically call the 'Penal Codes' – Sharia Law, to those who do not know. The idea that Sharia

Law could be enforced in opposition to the country's national constitution in the federal capital did not make any sense to me, so I took professional legal advice from a respected friend and colleague who would be in a position to know. His answer was short and simple.

> **"Actually, the Penal Code is supposed to be subject to the constitution, which could always be interpreted to supersede such provisions."**
> *Fifehan Ogunde PhD, Senior Legal Consultant, Wemimo Ogunde & Co.*

In other words, we can discount legal backing from the Sharia penal codes as the basis for Hajiya Safiya's FCT rape gang. At best, there is a measure of ambiguity about whether or not these penal codes can be enforced where they contradict the constitution directly, but there is simply no legal basis at all for having a gang of brutal rapists masquerading as a sort of morality police outfit, terrorising young women in their 20s and 30s across the nation's capital.

Thus in addition to merely being morally abominable, grotesque and disgusting, Hajiya Safiya's rape-enhanced war on Abuja's women is also plainly illegal. She is breaking the law and so she and her gang of morality rapists must be stopped and held to account immediately. In any case, the point is moot, because surely Sharia law does not prescribe rape as a punishment for boarding a keke or attending a birthday party or going for a night out with friends.

From a political perspective, what is playing out in Abuja right now at the behest of Safiya Umar and her colleagues is also more than just a group of officially-sanctioned gangsters organising an extortion racket, as is usually the case elsewhere in Nigeria. Hajiya Umar plainly fancies herself a champion of a notoriously parochial ethnoreligious elite with designs on remolding the Nigerian State and Nigerian society at large in the image of a terrified feudal society with a small everlasting elite and a sprawling, unquestioning everlasting underclass.

To this end, Hajiya Umar's SDS and their brutal AEPB enforcers are testing the waters through the blatant illegality of subjecting Nigeria's capital to an undemocratic pseudo-dictatorship and an accompanying culture of sexual violence to instill fear, shame and silence in a population that does not satisfy her cultural expectations. It is no coincidence that this is happening alongside the ongoing SARS menace because as with all wannabe dictators who have no capacity to lead independent, vocal and confident populations hungry for more democracy, the strategy is to break the spirit of the young people.

It is important to understand that kite-flying about so-called penal codes, AEPB-facilitated mass rapes, abductions, extortions and gratuitous violence are not mere by-products of Hajiya Umar's social cleansing campaign – they are the point. The policy direction of the SDS and the AEPB is now determined by a mafia with a blatant and undisguised cultural agenda seeking to modify Nigeria's federal capital into something closer in character to Gusau or Damaturu.

The good people of Gusau and Damaturu are no doubt happy enough with their societal arrangement, as the people of Benin, Jos, Lagos, Enugu, Port Harcourt, Ibadan and Abuja are with theirs. Nigeria is nothing if not a multicultural, multi-ethnic, multi religious and generally heterogeneous country. One of the best things about Abuja historically is that it is one of the few truly cosmopolitan melting pots in Nigeria, which is how it attracts Nigeria's best talent away from the afore-mentioned urban centres.

Using vicious sexual violence as a vehicle, Hajiya Safiya Umar and her co-travelers are slowly but deliberately destroying the social and cultural fabric of Nigeria's second most important city. This must be robustly challenged and blocked at every turn. Abuja is Nigeria's federal capital territory. It does not belong to Safiya Umar, neither does it belong to the gang of uniformed and civilian rapists she is willfully and knowingly empowering in pursuit of a parochial, anachronistic agenda. We need to remind people like Mrs. Umar that whether they like it or not, Nigeria is not – and can never be – the feudal society of their fantasies. My starting suggestion for doing this is simple: take a picture of her and thus demystify the ghost behind the rapists.

In so doing, we will once again reaffirm that Abuja belongs to all Nigerians from all 930,000+ square kilometre of this country, including Cynthia, Peace, Mercy, Judith, Patricia, Mary, and every other young Nigerian woman.

> **"I want Justice, if they're pursuing us in another country, they'd now be pursuing us in our own country also. We are Nigerians why will they be treating us like we don't deserve rights?"**
> *Judith*

II

THE FULL STORY OF NIGERIA'S UNFOLDING CORONAVIRUS SCANDAL

Employees of the Dangote Oil Refinery Company in Ibeju-Lekki, Lagos are currently in varying degrees of panic as a leaked internal email yesterday indicated that the company is dealing with a suspected case of COVID-19. A trusted source at the company who asked not to be named has confirmed that the patient in question – an Indian pipe fitter working at the giant petrochemical complex – is currently in isolation on site.

When I spoke to my source earlier today, I initially expected this to be yet another story of a Nigerian corporate? taking liberties with the lax regulatory environment to put its own interests first while flouting rules and putting people in danger. As I found out later, this goes well beyond Dangote Group or its internal health policy. This is a story about how Nigeria is facing a dire health emergency, driven by a perfect storm of incompetent governance, crass politicking, ignorance and corporate insularity.

Exhibit A: The Indian Pipe Fitter

Last week Thursday (March 12, 2020), a pipe fitter contracted to work at Dangote Refinery boarded a flight from Mumbai, India to Cairo, Egypt. After a brief stopover, he boarded another flight to Lagos, Nigeria where he was to resume work the following Monday. When he showed up at work on Monday however, something was wrong. He had a fever, a dry cough, a sore throat and significant breathing difficulty.

Dr. Avijit Singh, a Russian-trained surgeon with 10 years of experience in general surgery and practise across two continents, was the doctor on duty at the site clinic. He immediately suspected that the patient was infected with the coronavirus by virtue of his symptoms and his travel history (Cairo is a COVID-19 hotspot with over 150 known cases as at yesterday).

After isolating the patient, he fired off an email to the on-site safety officer, Akhil Kuniyil, detailing the incident with full disclosure of the patient's travel history, location and suspected diagnosis. It is unclear whether anyone at Dangote Refinery attempted to establish contact with the Nigeria Centre for Disease Control (NCDC), the Federal Ministry of Health or the Lagos State Ministry of Health after becoming aware of this information.

←   ⬇   🗑   ✉   ⋮

Safe Regards,
AKHIL KUNIYIL

Today was tomorrow . yesterday.
Don't wait . fulfill your (HSE) responsibilities - NOW!

-----Original Message-----
From: avijit singh [mailto:███████@yahoo.com]
Sent: 16 March 2020 03:19
To: Vishwanath Sir Onshore NV
Cc: Akhil Kuniyil
Subject: Suspected case of COVID -19

Dear Sir

       I would like to inform that we have a patient who came to our
clinic today morning with high temperature 38.5 c dry cough soar throat
difficulty in breathing.We are suspecting of Corona virus as he has recently
came from India.
Following are the details of the Patient:
Name of suspect: ███████████ Employee ID-62178
Nationality: Indian
Passport number: ███████
Job Title: ASSISTANT PIPE FITTER
Date of arrival in Nigeria: 12-03-2020
Port of Boarding : Mumbai, India. (Via cairo, Egypt) Flight and transit
information MS 969 12MAR BOMCAI 0250 0610 MS 875
12MAR CAILOS 0815 1335
Symptoms showing: he is having severe dry cough with high temperature and
breathing difficulties as reported.
Isolated Location: ████████████████ Dangote Refinery camp, Lekki
Freezone, Lagos, Nigeria.
Thanks & Regards
Dr.Avijit Singh

18

At press time, no information had been released by any of the concerned parties to address the building story. Staff members at the refinery meanwhile, got their hands on the communication between Dr. Singh and Mr. Kuniyil and according to my source, an unredacted version of the screenshot above has been circulating among refinery staff, their friends and families for more than 24 hours. My source further informed me that in addition to sitting on such critical information and stonewalling regulators as Dangote Refinery is in the habit of doing, certain practices and conditions on site may actually be aiding the possible spread of COVID-19.

He was especially keen to point out that despite the extant coronavirus threat, a temperature scanner was only installed on site yesterday, Monday, 16 March, 2020. The site meanwhile, employs hundreds of people who congregate every morning and then disperse back into Lagos every evening. In other words, Dangote Refinery has yet again ignored local and international HSE best practices and puts its workers at risk – only this time the risk extends beyond its workers. The sprawling Ibeju-Lekki Free Trade Zone is now effectively a brewing COVID-19 hotspot in Lagos with hundreds of potential disease vectors coming out of it every day.

Describing the internal chaos after the news of the suspected COVID-19 case leaked yesterday my source said:

"The temperature scanner was installed just yesterday. And, it created a severe bottleneck where many people have to cram into a small space to get screened daily, thus ensuring that the virus really goes round if one person has it."

The solution according to him, is for the entire complex to shut down operations until the threat blows over. The alternative he says, is to risk the daily temperature check that should counteract the spread of COVID-19, itself becoming a dispersion point for the virus. In his words:

"I guess it is a question of saving lives vs keeping the project moving."

Exhibit B: The Insecure Minister and the Unprepared Government

When NCDC Chair, Chikwe Ihekweazu, recently visited China to observe its coronavirus containment efforts as part of a capacity building exercise facilitated by the World Health Organisation, few might have thought of it as anything other than an objectively good thing. What better place for Nigeria's disease control czar to be than the epicentre of the global outbreak picking up useful information that could help Nigeria? One of those few however, turned out to be the Federal Minister of Health, Osagie Ehanire.

According to a source who is familiar with the matter, Ehanire was apparently unhappy that national and global attention was coming the way of Ihekweazu, who is technically his subordinate. Known to have gubernatorial ambitions in his native Edo State, Ehanire apparently sees the COVID-19 outbreak as the perfect staging point to build his political brand and come to the forefront of Edo's political consciousness. The fact that local and international media and multilateral bodies prefer to interact directly with the NCDC – without necessarily making reference to him – is a problem. Unfortunately, in this context of Nigeria's fight against a deadly pandemic, this petty clash of egos is now everybody's problem.

Rather than focusing some energy on coordinating efforts to fight the spread of the coronavirus, Ehanire has instead made it a point to put his face in front of every available camera and make it clear that he – not Ihekweazu – is the one in charge. Ihekweazu is no longer permitted to speak to the media independently about COVID-19, and he must now report to the Federal Ministry of Health and operate from there. In other words, the most important thing about the COVID-19 crisis in the eyes of the FMOH is that the world must know that it is the health minister's show, and his alone.

Last week, Ehanire took the most telling step to reclaiming his ostensibly lost glory and pushing his political agenda when he hosted a press conference to announce Nigeria's second COVID-19 case. The location of a press conference organised to make a nationwide health announcement? Benin City, Edo State.

While this was happening meanwhile, Nigeria's management capacity for COVID-19 was significantly lower than publicly claimed. It will be recalled that when the Italian index patient was identified and confined in Lagos, everyone concerned treated the story as evidence of preparedness with some even sounding triumphal. In reality what actually happened was that the subject self-presented and was diagnosed – the good news ended there.

Describing what happened next, my source says:

> **"The case in Lagos for instance took the intervention of the Italian ambassador for the patient to be moved. The place he was kept initially wasn't habitable. While govt. was on air claiming to have contained him in a hospital – he was literally abandoned at a poorly maintained facility, which is why Punch reported his attempted escape because he was dealing with mosquito bites."**

In the context of Nigeria's porous land borders and the up to 30-day asymptomatic incubation period of COVID-19, during which time it is infectious, nobody actually knows how many novel coronavirus cases are in Nigeria. While the FMOH and the NCDC engage in a pointless pissing contest, hundreds of thousands of Nigerians could currently be carrying the COVID-19 virus, without anything close to the required testing capacity to find out.

Prof. Akin Abayomi ✓
@ProfAkinAbayomi · **Follow**

Breaking! **#COVID19Lagos** Updates
If you are a passenger on flight BA 75
that arrived in Lagos on 13th March,
2020, stay at home and isolate
yourself for 14 days.
Call **@LSMOH** hotlines now;
08000corona, 08023169485,
08033565529,
08052817243, 08028971864,
08059758886, 08035387653

LAGOS STATE GOVERNMENT
MINISTRY OF HEALTH

#COVID19Lagos

11:12 AM · Mar 17, 2020

Read the full conversation on Twitter

♡ 3.8K   ○ Reply   ↑ Share

Read 766 replies

The Nigerian government strategy right now appears to be to cross both fingers, wait it out and hope. The NCDC has been shackled. Osagie Ehanire wants to be governor. Private corporations are managing the health crisis on their own – and possibly worsening it. The government at state and federal levels are broke and under-resourced. Ultimately, it would seem that any salvation from COVID-19, if it is to come, will be from our climate and our natural immune systems.

Nigerians once again, are on their own.

III

NIGERIA'S PROPOSED INFECTIOUS DISEASE ACT: PLAGIARISED AND DANGEROUS

Yesterday April 28, 2020, a piece of draft legislation that could permanently change the experience of Nigeria as we know it was quietly transmitted to members of the House of Representatives for consideration. On the surface, it is a somewhat innocuous bill – possibly even praiseworthy and necessary, but as has become the case in recent times, a closer examination of this bill reveals that it potentially creates a lot more problems than it purports to solve.

The Infectious Diseases Act is supposed to create a legal framework for the federal government to manage the special circumstances surrounding infectious disease outbreaks like the ongoing COVID-19 pandemic, which at last count had claimed 44 lives across Nigeria.

Sponsored by House Speaker, Femi Gbajabiamila, what the bill is supposed to do is provide an updated legislative basis for the government's anti-pandemic efforts, replacing the National Quarantine Act of 2004, which many have identified as the cause of least some of the FG's initial flat-footed response to COVID-19.

In reality, it potentially opens the door to a new set of legal and constitutional quagmires.

Also, it is almost entirely – word for word – plagiarised from the Singapore Infectious Diseases Act 1977.

Director-General or Unelected Dictator?

The first thing that quickly becomes clear about the bill is that it is not so much a bill about helping to save Nigerian lives from disease outbreaks as it is one about helping the Director-General of the Nigerian Centre for Disease Control (NCDC) and the Minister of Health become disproportionately and unjustifiably powerful.

Throughout the 44-page document, the term "Director General" appears 134 times – 10 more times than the word "disease."

At first the repeated emphasis on granting powers to the person of the NCDC DG appear justified by Sections 7 and 12, which give the DG the power to require that corpses of those who die of suspicious symptoms without confirmation must be properly autopsied, and that infected corpses must be disposed of in such a way as not to endanger public safety. Such clauses would – at least on paper – provide a resolution to scenarios such as that currently happening in Kano State, where for religious reasons, corpses of people who died of symptoms similar to COVID-19 victims are being hurriedly buried without autopsies and under unsafe circumstances.

Post-mortem examination

7. Where any person has died whilst being, or suspected of being, a case or carrier or contact of an infectious disease, the Director General may order a post-mortem examination of the body of that person for the purpose of —

(a) determining the cause or circumstances of the death of that person; or

(b) investigating into any outbreak or suspected outbreak of, or preventing the spread or possible outbreak of, that disease.

[...]

Wakes and disposal of corpses

12.—(1) Where any person has died whilst being, or suspected of being, a case or carrier or contact of an infectious disease, the Director General may by order —

(a) prohibit the conduct of a wake over the body of that person or impose such conditions as he thinks fit on the conduct of such wake; or

(b) impose such conditions as he thinks fit for the collection, removal and disposal of the body of that person.

(2) If any person contravenes any order under subsection (1) —

(a) that person shall be guilty of an offence; and

(b) any Health Officer may take such steps as may be necessary to ensure that the order is complied with, including entering any premises at any time without warrant and with such force as may be necessary to collect, remove and dispose of the body of the deceased person.

As with any other piece of legislation in Nigeria of course, whether it will be interpreted as superior to the Sharia penal code system of 12 Northern states and enforced accordingly, is anyone's guess.

The real problems with this bill becomes clear from Section 15, which states in part,

"The Minister may, for the purpose of preventing the spread or possible outbreak of an infectious disease, by notification in the Gazette declare any premises to be an isolation area…A person who leaves or attempts to leave or is suspected of having left an isolation area in contravention of an order under subsection (3) may be arrested without warrant by any police officer, or by any Health Officer authorised in writing in that behalf by the Director General."

Isolation area

15.—(1) The Minister may, for the purpose of preventing the spread or possible outbreak of an infectious disease, by notification in the Gazette declare any premises to be an isolation area.

(2) A notification under subsection (1) shall be effective until the expiration of such period as may be specified in the notification or until it is revoked by the Minister, whichever occurs first.

(3) The Director General may, in relation to an isolation area, by order —
(a) prohibit any person or class of persons from entering or leaving the isolation area without the permission of the Director General;
(b) prohibit or restrict the movement within the isolation area of any person or class of persons;
(c) prohibit or restrict the movement of goods;

9

(d) require any person or class of persons to report at specified times and places and submit to such medical examinations, answer such questions and submit to such medical treatment as the Director General thinks fit;
(e) authorise the destruction, disposal or treatment of any goods, structure, water supply, drainage and sewerage system or other matter within the isolation area known or suspected to be a source of infection; and
(f) prohibit, restrict, require or authorise the carrying out of such other act as may be prescribed.

The problematic phrase "without warrant," which gives law enforcement agents /agencies a free hand to arrest and detain without any proof of guilt whatsoever – and effectively removes a Nigerian citizen's constitutionally guaranteed right to assumed innocence and fair hearing – appears 14 different times in this bill. In the instance above, law enforcement officials are empowered to detain Nigerians on the mere suspicion of having been in a certain place, without the need for a single shred of evidence to back up their claims. In other words, Nigeria's famously disciplined, well-behaved and incorruptible police and paramilitary forces will be legally empowered to stop anyone anywhere, suspect them of having been in an isolation area, and detain them.

The ambiguously-worded clause immediately after gives even more cause for concern: "A Health Officer or a police officer may take any action that is necessary to give effect to an order under subsection 3." What does "action that is necessary" mean exactly? Does it mean indiscriminate stop-and-search actions? Does it mean shooting people "accidentally" as the lower ranks of the police are in the habit of doing? What are the real world Nigerian implications of giving sweeping, ambiguously-worded powers to poorly trained, power-drunk law enforcement officials with military grade firearms?

It gets worse. A lot worse actually.

Section 20 ends the right to free association through yet another sweeping, clumsily-worded clause that can be interpreted in just about any way whatsoever by the DG it empowers to prevent any kind of meting whatsoever as long as he determines in his subjective judgment that it somehow "increases the spread of an infectious disease."

Prohibition or restriction of meetings, gatherings and public entertainments

20.—(1) Where it appears to the Director General that the holding of any meeting, gathering or any public entertainment is likely to increase the spread of any infectious disease, the Director General may by order prohibit or restrict, subject to such conditions as he may think fit, for a period not exceeding 14 days, the meeting, gathering or public entertainment in any place.

(2) An order under subsection (1) may be renewed by the Director General from time to time for such period, not exceeding 14 days, as he may, by written notice, specify.

(3) Any person who holds, is present at or has taken part in any meeting, gathering or public entertainment in contravention of an order by the Director General under subsection (1) shall be guilty of an offence.

(4) A Health Officer or a police officer may take any action that is necessary to give effect to an order under subsection (1).

(5) Any person who is aggrieved by any order of the Director General under subsection (1) may, within 7 days from the date of the order, appeal to the Minister whose decision shall be final.

(6) Notwithstanding that any appeal under subsection (4) is pending, an order made by the Director General under subsection (1) shall take effect from the date specified by the Director, unless the Minister otherwise directs.

In practice, what this means is that the day a non-scientist or politically-motivated individual becomes DG, an unelected bureaucrat will then have the power to crack down on anything from political opposition meetings to anti-government protests whether there is a disease outbreak or not. The only condition is that the DG must find the gathering to be dangerous in his opinion. Since when was a right that appears on Page 1 of the 1999 constitution subject to the personal whims of an unelected public office holder?

Even more significantly, why is it the case that once of the most controversial provisions of the now-iced Social Media Bill has found its way into a bill about managing infectious diseases? In that bill, an unelected bureaucrat was given the sole power to hear legal appeals that must be submitted within a specific time period. Complainants were not entitled to hearing in a court, and the bureaucrat's decision was final. What is that abominable clause doing in a bill that is supposed to help Nigerians survive infectious disease outbreaks? What is this really about?

Still it gets worse.

According to Section 24, police officers now have the power to "apprehend and take" anyone in any public location who is "suffering from an infectious disease." A sore throat is an infectious disease. The common cold is an infectious disease. Does this clause mean that anyone who coughs in the general vicinity of a police officer stands to be arrested on suspicion of "having an infectious disease?" Why do police officers who are not trained medical personnel get to make the judgment about who has an "infectious disease" or not?

24. Apprehension of persons on the streets suffering from infectious diseases

Every enforcement officer, police officer or any authorized officer may apprehend and take, any person suffering from any infectious disease whom the officer finds on any street, public, place, shop or public transportation to a hospital.

16

25. Power of enforcement officer to order destruction of house, building or anything

(1) The enforcement officer may obtain an order of court to destroy any building in which a case of infectious disease has occurred, or of any article or thing which may be considered necessary in the interest of the public health.

(2) Any such order will be carried out in such manner and by such person as the enforcement officer may direct.

Somehow it still gets worse.

Point (e) under Section 55 lays out the framework for what is blatantly an assault on journalists and whistleblowers. The clause requires any person to provide any book, document, correspondence or information requested by the DG and it also gives the DG unrestricted power to enter and search any premises without the need for small matters like court orders. In other words, if the DG, his boss or any of his colleagues in office suspect that a journalist or whistleblower is about to go public with embarrassing information, there is now a legal basis for state-sanctioned thuggery to ensure that they are silenced.

PART VII
Enforcement

Powers of the Centre in dealing with outbreaks and suspected outbreaks of infectious diseases

55.—(1) For the purpose of investigating into any outbreak or suspected outbreak of an infectious disease or for the purpose of preventing the spread or possible outbreak of an infectious disease, the Director General or any authorised Health Officer may —

(a) at any time without warrant and with such force as may be necessary —

(i) enter, inspect and search any premises; or

(ii) stop, board, inspect and search any conveyance, in which the outbreak or suspected outbreak has taken place;

(e) require any person —

(i) to furnish any information within his knowledge; or

(ii) to produce any book, document or other record which may be in his custody or possession for inspection by the Director General or Health Officer and the making of copies thereof, or to provide the Director or Health Officer with copies of such book, document or other record, within such time and in such form or manner as the Director General or Health Officer may specify and may, if necessary, further require such person to attend at a specified time and place for the purposes of complying with sub-paragraph (i) or (ii);

For good measure, this is reiterated in section 56.

Powers of investigation

56.—(1) For the purposes of an investigation into an offence punishable under this Act, any police officer, or any Health Officer who is authorised in writing in that behalf by the Director-General may —

(a) require any person —

(i) to furnish any information within his knowledge; or

(ii) to produce any book, document or other record which may be in his custody or possession for inspection by the police officer or Health Officer and the making of copies thereof, or to provide the police officer or Health Officer with copies of such book, document or other record, and may, if necessary, further require such person to attend at a specified time and place for the purposes of complying with sub-paragraph (i) or (ii);

(b) at any time without warrant and with such force as may be necessary, stop, board, enter, inspect and search any premises or conveyance;

(c) take samples of or seize any substance or matter found in any premises or conveyance mentioned in paragraph (b); and

(d) seize any book, document or record produced under paragraph (a) or found in any premises or conveyance mentioned in paragraph (b).

(2) A statement made by any person giving evidence under subsection (1)(a) — (a) shall be reduced to writing and read over to him; and (b) shall, after correction (if any), be signed by him.

(3) Any person who, without reasonable excuse — (a) refuses or fails to comply with any requirement of a police officer or Health Officer under subsection (1); or (b) refuses to answer or gives a false answer to any question put to him by a police officer or Health Officer, shall be guilty of an offence.

(4) For the purposes of subsection (3), it is a reasonable excuse for a person to refuse or fail to furnish any information, produce any book, document or other record or answer any question if doing so might tend to incriminate him.

(5) For the purposes of subsection (1)(a)(i), where any document or record required by a police officer or Health Officer is kept in electronic form, then —
(a) the power of the police officer or Health Officer to require such document or record to be produced for inspection includes the power to require a copy of the document or record to be made available for inspection in legible form; and

(b) the power of the police officer or Health Officer to inspect such document or record includes the power to require any person on the premises in question to give the police officer or Health Officer such assistance as the police officer or Health Officer may reasonably require to enable him to inspect and make copies of the document or record in legible form or to make records of the information contained therein.

Section 58 contains possibly the worst clause in the entire document. Here, it is expressly stated that any police officer is empowered to arrest anyone without a warrant as long as "he has reason to believe…" In other words, the burden of proof is now on Nigerian citizens. We will all become guilty until proven innocent, which is yet another direct contravention of the 1999 constitution.

Powers of arrest

58.—(1) Any police officer, or any Health Officer authorised in writing in that behalf by the Director General, may arrest without warrant any person committing or who he has reason to believe has committed any offence under section 11(1), 20(2), 22(4), or 55(8).

(2) Subject to subsection (1), any police officer, or any Health Officer authorised in writing in that behalf by the Director-General, may arrest without warrant any person committing or who he has reason to believe has committed any offence under this Act if —

(a) the name and address of the person are unknown to him;

(b) the person declines to give his name and address;

(c) the person gives an address outside Nigeria; or

(d) there is reason to doubt the accuracy of the name and address if given.

The final coup-de-grace appears in Section 71 where it is stated that the DG and his enforcers in the police and paramilitary forces can never be held accountable for what they use these powers to do. The section reads: "No liability shall lie personally against the Director-General, any Health Officer, any Port Health Officer, any police officer or any authorised person who, acting in good faith and with reasonable care, does or omits to do anything in the execution or purported execution of this Act."

Obstruction of persons executing power, etc.
68. Any person who —
(a) in any way hinders or obstructs or assists in hindering or obstructing any person in the exercise of any power conferred by this Act; or
(b) being required to provide any information or documents under this Act (including as a condition of any order, notice or requirement made or given), provides any information or document which he knows to be false or misleading, shall be guilty of an offence.

General penalties
69. Any person guilty of an offence under this Act for which no penalty is expressly provided shall —
(a) in the case of a first offence, be liable on conviction to a fine not exceeding N100,000 or to imprisonment for a term not exceeding 6 months or to both; and
(b) in the case of a second or subsequent offence, be liable on conviction to a fine not exceeding N200,000 or to imprisonment for a term not exceeding 12 months or to both.

Offences triable by Magistrate's Court
70. Every offence under this Act may be tried by a Magistrate's Court, and that Court may, notwithstanding anything in the Criminal Procedure Code, award the full punishment with which the offence is punishable.

Protection from personal liability
71. No liability shall lie personally against the Director-General, any Health Officer, any Port Health Officer, any police officer or any authorised person who, acting in good faith and with reasonable care, does or omits to do anything in the execution or purported execution of this Act.

Immunity from liability for disclosure
72. No person commits an offence under any written law or any breach of confidence, incurs any civil liability or is liable to any disciplinary action by a professional body, by virtue merely of disclosing any information or providing any thing, in good faith and with reasonable care —

(a) in accordance with any requirement under this Act; or
(b) as authorised by the Director under section 61.

Policy Plagiarism Reveals Insincerity at Bill's Core

As mentioned at the outset, this bill is ripped off almost word for word from the Singapore Infectious Diseases Act of 1977. This could go some way to explaining why it is worded in such a combative and aggressive manner that takes almost zero notice of the assumed rights of citizens. Singapore at the time, was a fiercely authoritarian single party dictatorship led by Lee Kuan Yew. The fact that the existence of separation of powers and democratic freedoms exist in an electoral democracy like Nigeria appears completely lost on whoever 'Xeroxed' the Singaporean document.

Abatement of overcrowding

18. —(1) If, in the opinion of the Director, a building is so overcrowded as to expose the occupants thereof to the risk of infection by an infectious disease, the Director may, by notice in writing, direct the owner or occupier of the building to abate the overcrowding or to close the building or part thereof within the time specified in the notice.

(2) Any owner or occupier who fails to comply with a notice given to him by the Director under subsection (1) shall be guilty of an offence.

Abatement of overcrowding

17.—(1) If, in the opinion of the Director General, a building is so overcrowded as to expose the occupants thereof to the risk of infection by an infectious disease, he may, by written notice, direct the owner or occupier of the building to abate the overcrowding or to close the building or part thereof within the time specified in the notice.

(2) Any owner or occupier who fails to comply with a notice given to him by the Director under subsection (1) shall be guilty of an offence.

11

(3) When a building or any part thereof has been directed to be closed under subsection (1), any person who enters the building or any part thereof without the permission of the Director shall be guilty of an offence.

(4) Without prejudice to any proceedings under subsection (2), where a notice issued by the Director under subsection (1) has not been complied with, the Director, a Health Officer or a police officer may, without warrant and with such force as may be necessary, enter the building and take or cause to be taken such measures as are necessary to abate the overcrowding or to close the building or any part thereof, as specified in the notice.

[Excerpt from ILO Infectious Diseases Act 1977 (Amended 2009)]

(3) When a building or any part thereof has been directed to be closed under subsection (1), any person who enters the building or any part thereof without the permission of the Director General shall be guilty of an offence.

(4) Without prejudice to any proceedings under subsection (2), where a notice issued by the Director General under subsection (1) has not been complied with, the Director General, a Health Officer or a police officer may, without warrant and with such force as may be necessary, enter the building and take or cause to be taken such measures as are necessary to abate the overcrowding or to close the building or any part thereof, as specified in the notice.

[Excerpt from Draft Infectious Diseases Act 2020]

Notice anything?

Treatment of premises or vessel

12. —(1) The Director may, by notice in writing, require the owner or occupier of any premises or vessel to cleanse or disinfect it in the manner and within the time specified in the notice.

(5.2003)

(2) Any owner or occupier who fails to comply with the requirements of the notice served under subsection (1) shall be guilty of an offence.

(3) Without prejudice to any proceedings under subsection (2), where a notice issued by the Director under subsection (1) has not been complied with, a person authorised in that behalf by the Director may, without warrant and with such force as may be necessary, enter the premises or vessel to which the notice relates and take or cause to be taken such measures as have been specified in the notice.

(4.2002)

(4) The cost and expenses incurred by the Director under subsection (3) shall be paid by the person in default and may be recovered as a debt due to the Government.

Destruction and disposal of infected animals, food and water

13. —(1) The Director may order the destruction of any animal and the disposal of

Singaporean Original

Treatment of premises or vessel

10.—(1) The Director General may, by written notice, require the owner or occupier of any premises or vessel to cleanse or disinfect it in the manner and within the time specified in the notice.

(2) Any owner or occupier who fails to comply with the requirements of the notice served under subsection (1) shall be guilty of an offence.

(3) Without prejudice to any proceedings under subsection (2), where a notice issued by the Director General under subsection (1) has not been complied with, a person authorised in that behalf by the Director General may, without warrant and with such force as may be necessary, enter the premises or vessel to which the notice relates and take or cause to be taken such measures as have been specified in the notice.

(4) The cost and expenses incurred by the Centre under subsection (3) shall be paid by the person in default and may be recovered as a debt due to the Government.

Destruction and disposal of infected animals, food and water

11.—(1) The Director General may order the destruction of any animal and the disposal of any food or water wherever found if he considers such animal, food or water to be a source for the transmission of an infectious disease.

(2) Any person who fails to comply with an order made by the Director General under subsection (1) shall be guilty of an offence.

(3) Without prejudice to any proceedings under subsection (2), where an order made by the Director General under subsection (1) has not been complied with, the Director General, a Health Officer or a police officer may —

Nigerian Copy

And this…

Wakes and disposal of corpses

14. —(1) Where any person has died whilst being, or suspected of being, a case or carrier or contact of an infectious disease, the Director may by order —
(a) prohibit the conduct of a wake over the body of that person or impose such conditions as he thinks fit on the conduct of such wake; or
(b) impose such conditions as he thinks fit for the collection, removal and disposal of the body of that person.
[7/2008]

(2) If any person contravenes any order under subsection (1) —
(a) that person shall be guilty of an offence; and
(b) any Health Officer may take such steps as may be necessary to ensure that the order is complied with, including entering any premises at any time without warrant and with such force as may be necessary to collect, remove and dispose of the body of the deceased person.
[7/2008]

(3) Any costs and expenses incurred by a Health Officer under subsection (2) (b) shall be borne by the person in default and may be recovered as a debt due to the Government.
[7/2008]

Isolation of certain persons

15. —(1) The Director may order any person who is, or is suspected to be, a case or carrier or contact of an infectious disease to be detained and isolated in a hospital or other place for such period of time and subject to such conditions as the Director may determine.
[7/2008]

(2) The Director may order any person who is, or is suspected or continues to be suspected to be, a case or carrier or contact of an infectious disease, or who has recently recovered from or been treated for such disease, to remain and to be isolated and (if necessary) be treated, in his own dwelling place; —

Disinfection and treatment of vessel and vehicle

32. —(1) The Director or a Health Officer authorised by the Director may, in his discretion, order the disinfection and treatment of the clothes and personal effects of any infected person arriving in Singapore.
[4/2002; S/2003]

(2) Any vessel or vehicle which has conveyed an infected person shall be cleansed, disinfected or treated in such manner as may be directed by the Director or a Health Officer authorised by the Director.
[4/2002; S/2003]

Arrival of infected ships

33. —(1) An infected ship shall anchor at a quarantine anchorage unless otherwise directed by a Port Health Officer and shall remain there until it has been granted pratique by a Port Health Officer.
(2) An infected ship lying within the waters of Singapore shall show the appropriate quarantine signal prescribed by regulations unless otherwise directed by a Port Health Officer.
(3) No person shall board or disembark from the ship while it lies at a quarantine anchorage, without obtaining the prior written permission of a Port Health Officer.
(4) No baggage, cargo or article may be discharged from a ship while it lies at a quarantine anchorage without the prior written permission of a Port Health Officer.
(5) Any master or any other person who contravenes this section shall be guilty of an offence and shall be liable on conviction to a fine not exceeding $10,000 or to imprisonment for a term not exceeding 12 months or to both.

Unauthorised boarding or disembarking from infected vessel

34. —(1) The master of any infected vessel shall while it is subject to quarantine —
(a) prevent and, if necessary, detain any person disembarking from the vessel without being authorised by a Port Health Officer;
(b) detain any person from Singapore who without the permission of a Port Health Officer boards the vessel;
(c) deliver any person detained to a Port Health Officer;
(d) prevent any baggage or cargo from being discharged from the vessel; and
(e) prevent any rodent from leaving or entering the vessel.
(2) A master who fails to comply with any of the provisions of subsection (1) and any person aiding or abetting a master shall be guilty of an offence and shall be liable on

Wakes and disposal of corpses

12.—(1) Where any person has died whilst being, or suspected of being, a case or carrier or contact of an infectious disease, the Director General may by order —
(a) prohibit the conduct of a wake over the body of that person or impose such conditions as he thinks fit on the conduct of such wake; or
(b) impose such conditions as he thinks fit for the collection, removal and disposal of the body of that person.

(2) If any person contravenes any order under subsection (1) —
(a) that person shall be guilty of an offence; and
(b) any Health Officer may take such steps as may be necessary to ensure that the order is complied with, including entering any premises at any time without warrant and with such force as may be necessary to collect, remove and dispose of the body of the deceased person.

(3) Any costs and expenses incurred by a Health Officer under subsection (2)(b) shall be borne by the person in default and may be recovered at a debt due to the Government.

Isolation of certain persons

11.—(1) The Director General may order any person who is, or is suspected to be, a case or carrier or contact of an infectious disease to be detained and isolated in a hospital or other place for such period of time and subject to such conditions as the Director General may determine.

(2) The Director General may order any person who is, or is suspected or continues to be suspected to be, a case or carrier or contact of an infectious disease, or who has recently recovered from or been treated for such disease, to remain and to be isolated and (if necessary) be treated, in his own dwelling place — (a) for such period of time as may be necessary for the protection of the public; and (b) subject to such conditions as the Director General may consider necessary for this purpose.

(3) Where the person who is to be isolated under subsection (1) or (2) is a minor, the Director may order the parent or guardian of the minor —
(a) to take the minor, within the time specified in the order, to the place to which he is to be isolated; or
(b) to ensure that the minor remains in isolation in his own dwelling place, for such period of time and subject to such conditions as may be specified by the Director

Disinfection and treatment of vessel and vehicle

32.—(1) The Director General or an authorised Health Officer may, in his discretion, order the disinfection and treatment of the clothes and personal effects of any infected person arriving in Nigeria.

(2) Any vessel or vehicle which has conveyed an infected person shall be cleansed, disinfected or treated in such manner as may be directed by the Director or an authorised Health Officer.

Arrival of infected ships

33.—(1) An infected ship shall anchor at a quarantine anchorage unless otherwise directed by a Port Health Officer and shall remain there until it has been granted pratique by a Port Health Officer.

(2) An infected ship lying within the waters of Nigeria shall show the appropriate quarantine signal prescribed by regulations unless otherwise directed by a Port Health Officer.

19

(3) No person shall board or disembark from the ship while it lies at a quarantine anchorage, without obtaining the prior written permission of a Port Health Officer.

(4) No baggage, cargo or article may be discharged from a ship while it lies at a quarantine anchorage without the prior written permission of a Port Health Officer.

(5) Any master or any other person who contravenes this section shall be guilty of an offence and shall be liable on conviction to a fine not exceeding N1,000,000 or to imprisonment for a term not exceeding 12 months or to both.

This too…

Singaporean Original

Nigerian Copy

And this as well…

It goes on and on like this for practically all 44 pages (the Singaporean original legislation has 43 pages). It is page after page of authoritarianism from Southeast Asia with "Singapore" occasionally 'Tippexed' out and "Nigeria" scrawled over it. In fact when you run the draft legislation through a plagiarism checker, Nigeria's proposed legislation has an originality score of just 2 percent against the Singaporean document it was plagiarised from.

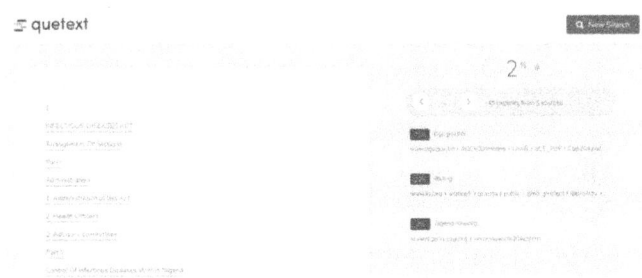

If this were a school essay, one would get hauled before a disciplinary committee.

It might be tempting to see the funny side of this and chalk it up to the usual intellectual vacuity that Nigeria's government is renowned for. In a country that is currently led by a party that plagiarised its entire manifesto in the most recent elections – famously leaving in a reference to "American security" in the poorly-edited document – policymakers phoning it in by copying other people's work is hardly strange news. After all the party had its plagiarised manifesto publicly exposed – and it still won its election.

In this case however, someone specifically sought out an obnoxiously worded Infectious Diseases Act from a notoriously dictatorial country and did a Ctrl+G (find and replace) function on it to change the term "director" to "Director General" without making much of an attempt to change anything else. This indicates that the only goal behind this proposed legislation is specifically to expand the spectre of unaccountable, unelected dictatorship in Nigeria, and in the process remake the country as we know it in the authoritarian image of Singapore.

Just with none of the infrastructure and economic growth.

This means that this is not mere laziness or lack of imagination, though those are certainly part of the story. The bill is part of a directed and consistent campaign that started in 2015 to reduce the civil rights and liberties of Nigerians, especially their right to court hearings and their freedom of speech. Hiding under the cloak of yet another piece of boring, plagiarised legislation, there is a concerted and unmistakable effort to turn the clock back on Nigeria's democracy.

Analysis of Draft Bill

A few months ago, two pieces of legislation (the so-called 'Hate Speech' and 'Social media' bills) created an uproar when it emerged that if passed, their clauses would effectively end Nigerian civil rights as we know them. Due to the sustained public pushback, the bills were put on ice until such a time as their sponsors could attempt once again to bypass public outrage and sneak them into law. This bill is that attempt.

Not only will this bill effectively end the constitutionally guaranteed freedom of movement and freedom of association under the fraudulent guise of "public health," this bill also goes after property rights, giving an unelected DG and his unelected boss at the Health Ministry power to commandeer and expropriate private property with brazen audacity and on a scale that has not been seen in Nigeria since the days of military dictatorship.

If this bill is passed, journalists and whistleblowers will also be endangered, as it empowers the NCDC DG and health minister to use law enforcements to seize whatever information is deemed important in fighting an infectious disease. Information such as, for example the sources I exchanged correspondence with before recently publishing a story on the Health Ministry's lack of preparedness for the COVID-19 pandemic, which the Ministry found embarrassing. If this bill is passed, the act of writing and publishing such stories can legally be interpreted as an offense, and journalists will then be required to compromise the anonymity and personal safety of their sources, which would effectively end whatever remains of objective public interest journalism in Nigeria.

Most importantly, this bill automatically criminalises every Nigerian going about their legitimate daily business by making them guilty until pronounced innocent by the subjective judgment of an unelected DG – instead of a court. Under the guise of fighting infectious diseases, this bill will reintroduce mass surveillance to Nigeria and effectively end the rights to assumed innocence, fair hearing before a competent court of law and **habeas corpus** – the trifecta of legal principles that prevent Executive overreach and provide a framework for the freedoms inherent in democratic countries. Instead, Nigeria will become a stop-and-search police state with subjective, warrantless arrests, zero recourse to fair hearing in court, indefinite detention and legal appeals being heard by unelected civil dictators instead of qualified judges.

Giving his opinion of the bill, human rights activist and Executive Director, Adopt a Goal for Development Initiative, Ariyo-Dare Atoye said:

"The infectious disease act is more of a punitive bill than a draft law for addressing infectious diseases. This bill tends to confer absolute powers and illegal authorities on a Director-General, including power to "arrest without warrant." See section 58. The bill was written with a mindset that is both colonial and autocratic. The only thing the drafter of the bill failed to do out of "shame" is not to have "as appropriate" in the context of its overreach – used the nomenclature of Governor-General for the DG. See sections 20, 25 and other punitive provisions in the bill

Not done with its scrambling for absolute control, the bill also confers an obnoxious power on the Supervising

Minister in Section 20 (5) "Any person who is aggrieved by any order of the Director General under subsection (1) may, within 7 days from the date of the order, appeal to the Minister whose decision shall be final." This is a usurpation of the powers of the Judiciary, especially the Supreme Court which has the final authority of law in the country.

It will be too early to call for the death of the bill even though it is terribly defective with several punitive measures that give the DG the powers to act like a colonial Czar. However, I will like to appeal to Nigerians to let us critically review and appraise this draft law and see whether it could be exorcised of its illegal powers and provisions. The bill bears the signature of a draft that originated from a communist republic."

IV

THE DEBT THAT COULD SPARK A DIPLOMATIC ROW: INSIDE INDIAN WORKERS' 4-YEAR BATTLE FOR THEIR ENTITLEMENTS WITH GLOBACOM

For decades, there has been a mutually beneficial relationship between India and Nigeria in terms of providing highly skilled manpower to build businesses at a significantly reduced cost, relative to what it would take to bring a European or an American to Nigeria. Nigerian FMCGs, building contractors, telecom firms and professional consultancies have long looked eastward to the world's largest democracy for skilled personnel who are relatively affordable and can absorb the inconveniences of living in a developing country.

There is also an old, extensive and powerful Indian business community in Nigeria dating back to the post-independence era, with some Indian-Nigerian families tracing back their time in the country up to 3 generations. Typically, when a story about Indians and Nigerian labour issues comes up, it tends to go somewhat along the lines of "rich foreigners mistreat Nigerians in their own country," which generally turns out to be true as often as it does not. It would hardly occur to anyone that such mistreatment could also go in the opposite direction.

When an Indian national reached out to me last month with a story about 40 Indian ex-Globacom personnel allegedly stiffed of their wages and entitlements, and a subsequent half-decade of international shenanigans and intrigues to avoid paying them including dodging the Nigerian court system and being effectively deported from India on at least one occasion, it seemed like something out of a movie. On the Nollywood side, here is an uber-rich 'Aka Gum' and his willing henchmen doing everything from making false written promises to skipping court appearances to get out of paying their debts.

On the Bollywood side, here is a small group of brave underdogs trying to fight injustice meted out by a wealthy man using nothing more than correspondence with the Indian civil service and belief in the ethics of a foreign journalist they have never met. This unlikely story somehow brings together elements of courtroom drama, political drama and police chase thriller. How could anyone not be intrigued?

Act 1: Billionaire vs Exploited Indian Workers

With a personal fortune estimated at $7.7bn by Forbes in February 2020, Globacom CEO Michael Adenuga Jr. (GCON) is very unlikely to be hurting for cash. His empire includes a majority stake in Globacom, a 20 percent stake in Julius Berger, a 5 percent stake in Sterling Bank, a majority stake in Conoil and real estate holdings worth billions of Naira among many other assets and holdings. Backing from this kind of wealth makes it near-impossible to hold his businesses to account if they act in bad faith, but that is exactly what 40 Indian nationals who used to be employed as expatriate staff at Globacom are trying to do.

Led by Alex James Murikan, an entrepreneur in Chennai, India, who worked as a General Manager at Globacom between 2010 and 2015, this group of employees is doing everything they can to draw attention to what they say is Adenuga's refusal to authorise payment of their wages and accumulated paid leave entitlements before they were laid off on October 23, 2015. Having worked at Globacom, typically for 5 to 8 years, their contracts were not renewed in 2015 and they returned to India having received letters stating that they would be paid all that they were due.

Five years later, those entitlements are still being owed despite several parleys between the ex-staff and the company. On at least one occasion as far back as 2016, after the ex-employees got the Indian High Commission, Abuja involved in the matter, official communication from Globacom's Head of HR came in, promising that payment was being processed and they would receive their entitlements shortly.

Four years after this email was sent, it would seem that either the company was lying or Globacom must have the slowest processing speed in the world, no pun intended. Here is Alex telling his story in his own words:

"As per Company policy, we are entitled to 28 days paid leave every year. Many of us have unutilized leave balance which also needs to be paid. The Full final settlement includes notice pay & accumulated leave balance. Many letters, emails, phone calls have been made to remind Globacom of settling our dues pending for more than 16 months. Recently, reminders have also gone to top officials.

These include Mr. Adewale Sangowawa (Executive Director, HR), Mrs. Gladys Talabi (ED, Legal), Mr. Bisi Kolesho (ED), Mr. Mike Jituboh (ED), Mr. Bjas Murthy (Commercial Officer), Mr. Sanjib Roy (Technical Officer), and Charles Jenarious (Communications Manager), however we have not received any favorable response yet from them. After we requested an intervention from the Indian High Commission, Abuja we then received acknowledgement from HR head, Mr. Femi Kolawole. However no payment has been received as of yet."

Olufemi Kolawole · 3rd

Globacom Nigeria Limited

HR Administrator at Globacom Nigeria Limited

Nigeria · 20 connections · Contact info

Experience

HR Administrator

Globacom Nigeria Limited

May 2013 – Present · 7 yrs 2 mos

Something that kept on recurring through my several conversations with Alex and his colleagues was the inference that not every senior person at Glo necessarily agreed with their treatment, but their hands were tied without authorisation from the very top. As long as the Chairman (Mr. Adenuga) refused to sign off on such outgoings, they would simply be left unpaid and there was nothing anybody could do about it.

Glo, essentially could well be the world's biggest one-man business operation.

Act 2: Flashback Cutaway Scene

Researching Mike Adenuga's business dealings over the years, a clear and unmistakable pattern of similar behaviour emerges. In 2016, it emerged that Conoil and another business he owns called Belbop were being pursued by several creditors including Baker Hughes, Total and British oil firm Vitol over debts totalling $140.5 million. Baker Hughes eventually lodged a winding up petition against Belbop at the Federal High Court in Ikoyi, Lagos, and an interim injunction on Belbop's company accounts was placed pending resolution of the suit.

Just as Glo's Indian ex-staff were promised their entitlements after a parley with senior figures at the company only for it to go back on its word without explanation, Total also found itself on the wrong end of this behaviour in 2015. Premium Times reported in 2016 that a meeting between Conoil and Total resulted in an agreement for Conoil to pay its $28.5 million debt to the French oil major which was developing the OML 136 gas field on its behalf. Instead, Conoil inexplicably refused to pay up and work stopped on the development, leading to lost jobs and lost potential investment.

In May 2016, Globacom's Lagos headquarters was sealed by the FIRS over alleged unpaid VAT totalling N24.3 billion. Going back to 2010, a N2.4 billion loan taken from Wema Bank by Adenuga's Covenant

Apartment Complex Limited turned into a bad loan after the company did not service it, and the Asset Management Corporation of Nigeria (AMCON) was forced to buy the bad debt in line with its goal of maintaining stability in the Nigerian financial system.

Going further back to 2009, Adenuga's Continental Oil and Gas and Conoil both found themselves embroiled in a tax dispute with the Federal Inland Revenue Service (FIRS), which claimed that they owed the government a total of $610 million in unremitted taxes. EFCC documents leaked in September 2016 also revealed that Conoil had failed to remit the sum of N1.03 billion to the government after being allocated petroleum products for distribution by the Pipelines and Products Marketing Company (PPMC).

There are several more stories like this about business entities linked to Adenuga, some confirmed and others little more than rumours. What is evident is that at every point in the story of Adenuga's business dealings over the past decade, there has been what is beginning to look like a pattern of bad faith indebtedness on the part of an individual who could at any point write a cheque worth the total value of his debts if he so wished.

Final Act: Mumbai Police, Polite Deportation and Dodging Courts

Driven to the wall and seemingly out of options due to Adenuga's famous intransigence, Alex and his colleagues decided to hit the nuclear button and write to Indian political, diplomatic and law enforcement authorities to see what could be done. In December 2016, the office of Indian Prime Minister Nanendra Modi officially acknowledged receipt of their complaint

09/06/2016	: Grievance Status

Status as on 09 Jun 2016

Registration Number	: PMOPG/E/2016/0199602
Name Of Complainant	: Alex James Murikan
Date of Receipt	: 09 Jun 2016
Received by	: Prime Ministers Office
Officer name	: Shri Ambuj Sharma
Officer Designation	: Under Secretary (Public)
Contact Address	: Public Wing
	5th Floor, Rail Bhawan
	New Delhi110011
Contact Number	: 011-23386447
e-mail	: ambuj.sharma38@nic.in
Grievance Description	Back Ground: • We are around 40(list attached) of us who were employed in Globacom. Nigeria have been working since last 7-8 years. • As per Company policy , we are entitled to 28 days paid leave every year • Our services were terminated last september.27th 2015 issued letters that we would be paid in lieu for the notice • Many of us have unutilized leave balance which also needs to be paid. The Full final settlement include notice pay accumulated leave balance. • Many letters phone calls have be made to remind Globacom of settling our dues pending for the last 7 months. recently, reminders have also gone to the officials, however we have no response from them. • we have sent letters to PGE, MC Luther last month after which we ha acknowledgements from Globacom • However no payment has been received as of yet • Globacom comes every 3 months to recruit Indians yet they have not paid former emloyees their dues Way Forward. we request a letter to be sent to the management (List attached) reminding that dues need to be paid to all of us at the earliest with a call to action .
Current Status	RECEIVED THE GRIEVANCE

Status as on 07 Dec 2016

Registration Number	: PMOPG/E/2016/0557120
Name Of Complainant	: Alex James Murikan
Date of Receipt	: 07 Dec 2016
Received by	: Prime Ministers Office
Officer name	: Shri Ambuj Sharma
Officer Designation	: Under Secretary (Public)
Contact Address	: Public Wing
	5th Floor, Rail Bhawan
	New Delhi 110011
Contact Number	: 011-23386447
e-mail	: ambuj.sharma38@nic.in
Grievance Description	pending from June 2016 Back Ground : • We are around 40(list attached) of us who were employed in Globacom. Nigeria have been working since last 51/2 years • As per Company policy , we are entitled to 28 days paid leave every year • Our services were terminated last September,27th 2015 issued letters that we would be paid in lieu for the notice • Many of us have unutilized leave balance which also needs to be paid. The Full final settlement include notice pay accumulated leave balance. • Many letters phone calls have be made to remind Globacom of settling our dues pending for the last 7 months. recently, reminders have also gone to the officials, however we have no response from them. • we have sent letters to PGE, MC Luther last month after which we ha acknowledgements from Globacom • However no payment has been received as of yet • Globacom comes every 3 months to recruit Indians yet they have not paid former employees their dues Way Forward: we request a letter to be sent to the management (List attached) reminding that dues need to be paid to all of us at the earliest with a call to action
Current Status	RECEIVED THE GRIEVANCE

They also reported Glo to the Indian Ministry of External Affairs, which felt strongly enough about it to send a distinctly passive-aggressive official letter to Glo, requesting the company to settle its obligations to its ex-staff and threatening it with police action against visiting Glo officials if it did not do so.

एम. सी. लूथर
M.C. LUTHER

सयुक्त सचिव
एवं उत्प्रवासी महासरक्षक
विदेश मंत्रालय
भारत सरकार
अकबर भवन, चाणक्यपुरी,
नई दिल्ली-110 021
भारत
Joint Secretary
& Protector General of Emigrants
Ministry of External Affairs
Government of India
Akbar Bhawan, Chanakyapuri,
New Delhi-110 021
INDIA

D.O. No. D.O. No. C-13019/189/2016-OE-II

4 January, 2016

Dear Mr. Sangowawa Adewale,

    I am constrained to point out that there are about 40 Indian employees of M/s. Globacom Limited whose dues are pending for settlement over last 16 months. Some of them have approached us requesting for taking up the matter with Globacom and have been regularly following up with us. It has been reported that Mr. Tony Ighalo and few other officials of M/s Globacom are currently on visit to New Delhi, Mumbai and Bangalore for conducting further interviews for overseas recruitment to Globacom.

    You may be aware that for carrying out overseas recruitment, the Foreign Employer are required to get Demand Letter duly attested by the nearest Indian Mission. This requirement is mandatory and any non-compliance of it is a violation of the provisions of Sections 10 and 24 of the Emigration Act, 1983, of India.

    Accordingly, the concerned Police authorities of New Delhi, Mumbai and Bengalure have been informed for taking appropriate action against visiting officials of M/s. Globecom and appropriate actions have been taken by the Police authorities.

    We are also requesting our Mission in Nigeria to scrutinize closely all visa applications of M/s Globacom before the same as granted, especially for overseas recruitment from India.

    In view of the above, I would request you to please have the matter of pending dues of these 40 Indian employees settled at the earliest (as per list enclosed). We look forward to an early response in the matter.

Regards,

Yours Sincerely,

(M. C. Luther)

Mr.Sangowawa Adewale
Director, HR-International recruitment
M/s Globacom Limited
Nigeria
sangowawa.adewale@gloworld.com
Mobile +234-80555770200

Copy to:

i)   Mr. Kaisar Alam, Deputy High Commissioner, High commission of India, Abuja, Nigeria. Dcm.abuja@mea.gov.in

ii) Mr.Mike Jituboh, Executive Director, M/s Globacom Limited, mike.jituboh@gloworld.com Mobile +2348055577777

iii) Ms.Bella Disu, Executive Director, M/s Globacom Limited, bella.disu@gloworld.com Mobile +234-7055559995

iv) Mr.OlabisiKolesho, Executive Director, M/s Globacom Limited, olabisi.kolesho@gloworld.comMobile +234-78055572400

v)   Ms.Gladys Talabi, Executive Director, M/s Globacom Limited, gladys.talabi@gloworld.com Mobile +234-78055573333

Not even a chillingly worded letter from a nuclear armed government was enough to convince Glo to pay up, however, and as Alex and several sources confirmed, Glo continued to plan its twice-yearly recruitment visit to India by senior HR officials. According to documents I sighted, one Mr. Tony Ighalo and another Glo employee simply identified as Mr. Donnie arrived in Delhi, India on December 17, 2016, which our little band of outlaws got wind of. They immediately notified the Indian Ministry of Internal Affairs, which promptly dispatched a letter to Delhi police instructing them to arrest the Globacom officials on charges of Cheating and Violating immigration rules by recruiting Indians without a valid license.

एम. सी. लूथर
M.C. LUTHER

D.O. No. C-13019/169/2016-OE-II

महावर सचिव
एवं उत्प्रवासी महानिदेशक
विदेश मंत्रालय
भारत सरकार, चाणक्यपुरी
नई दिल्ली-110 021
Joint Secretary
& Protector General of Emigrants
Ministry of External Affairs
Government of India
Akbar Bhawan, Chanakyapuri
New Delhi-110 021
Dated the 18th December, 2016

Dear Ravinder,

We have been approached by Mr. Alex James Murkun alleging that M/s. Globacom of Nigeria has not paid their dues. Mr. Alex has informed today that Mr. Tony Ignalo, Mr. Sangowawa Adeware and Mr. Donnie of M/s. Globacom have again arrived in New Delhi for making overseas recruitment. A copy of his email of today is enclosed which also gives details of their stay in New Delhi, along with photograph of Mr. Tony.

2. As per requirements, for carrying out overseas recruitment, the Foreign Employer are required to get Demand Letter etc. duly attested by the Indian Diplomatic Mission abroad. And, if a recruitment agency in India is involved that agency has to be registered under Section 10 of Emigration Act, 1983. Those who do not comply the above and still engage in overseas recruitment activities are not authorized to carry out overseas recruitment business without obtaining a valid Registration Certificate. This requirement is mandatory and any contravention of the same is an offence under Section 10 and 24 of the Emigration Act, 1983.

3. It has been alleged by around 40 Indian emigrants that M/s Globacom, Nigeria have cheated them and their dues have not been paid for more than seven months. Though they have already lodged complaints against M/s Globacom regarding cheating and non-settlement of pending dues, still they are going ahead for fresh recruitments in India. It is imperative that these foreigners should be arrested on the charges of violation of provisions of relevant Sections of Indian Penal Code and also violation of Sections 10 and 24 of the Emigration Act, 1983. We have received credible information that these illegal recruiters of M/s. Globacom have checked in hotel The Lalit, Barakhamba Road, New Delhi today and likely to stay for next 3-4 days only.

4. As the above foreigners do not meet the above requirement for carrying out overseas recruitment activities, you are requested to kindly get the above illegal recruiters arrested immediately and have the matter thoroughly investigated.

With kind regards,

Yours sincerely,
(M.C. LUTHER)

Shri Ravinder Singh Yadav
Joint Commissioner of Police (Crime)
Delhi Police
New Delhi

Encl: As above

Room No. 1013-14, 10th Floor, Akbar Bhavan, New Delhi. Phone: +91-11-26874250, Fax No.: +91-11-24197964
Email: pge@mea.gov.in

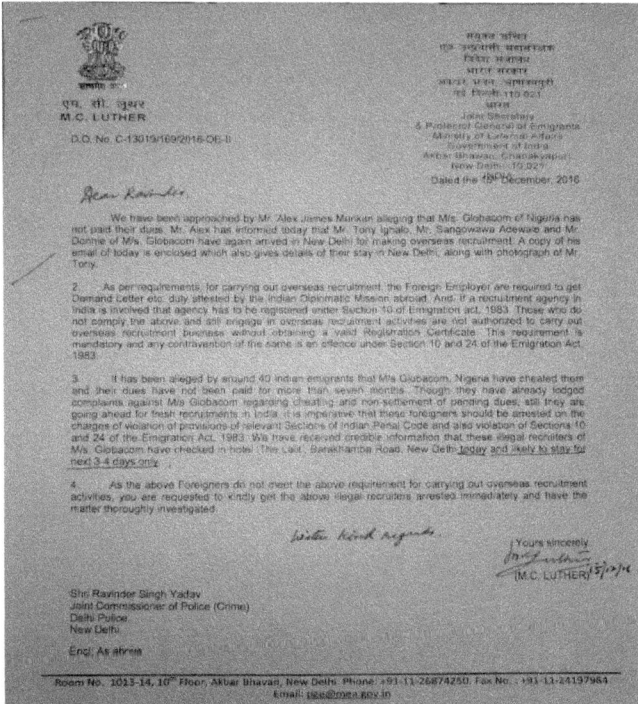

Incredibly, the two Glo personnel somehow managed to slip through the Delhi police net and on December 24, 2016, they arrived in Mumbai to carry out their recruitment assignment. Again, the MEA was notified and it promptly issued a letter to the Mumbai police ordering their arrest.

This time, they were successfully nabbed, and upon detailed interrogation, the police discovered that they had traveled to India on visiting visas instead of business visas, which violates India's Emigration Act. For whatever reason, the police decided to let them off on the condition that all interviews for expatriate recruitment would be suspended. They were also told that they would only be allowed to recruit in India again if they produced the proper documentation and proof that the dues and settlements of the 40 workers in question had been paid.

Describing what happened next, Alex says,

"A group of ex-Glo employees reached out to Tony & Donnie with the objective of reaching an amicable solution, however they were not in a position to commit anything as directives come from the chairman in Lagos. They also mentioned that they intended to continue with the recruitment process notwithstanding the communications from Indian police & Mumbai MEA. On 30th December, 2016 they left for Bangalore and based on our complaint the Bangalore police reached the venue at Taj, Vivanta, and instructed the duo to desist from recruiting/interviewing. They left Bangalore on 3rd January, 2017 and reached Delhi, and were met by the police in their Hotel at The Royal Plaza CP. They eventually left the country on 5th January 2017."

Or to put it bluntly, they were politely asked to leave the country.

Since then, the group of Indian ex-Glo employees has taken several alternate measures to get justice. At least two cases have been filed at the National Industrial Court in Ikoyi, Lagos, and in both cases the judgment was in favour of the complainants. Globacom however, failed to appear in court both times and has appealed the judgments.

IN THE NATIONAL INDUSTRIAL COURT OF NIGERIA
IN THE LAGOS JUDICIAL DIVISION
HOLDEN AT LAGOS

BEFORE HIS LORDSHIP HON. JUSTICE J.D. PETERS

DATE: MONDAY 23RD OCTOBER, 2017.   SUIT NO. NICN/LA/162/2017

Between

MR. SUBIR BANERJEE
....   Claimant
        And
GLOBACOM LIMITED   Defendant

Appearances
Claimant Attorney Present
Defendant Absent
Olawale Balogun for the Claimant

Balogun
Both Defendant and Counsel are not in Court. It is to hear pending application. There has been no appearance entered for Defence. There is a pending Notice of Preliminary Objection before the Court by Defendant. I pray the Court to strike same out

Court
Defendant is not in Court today to move its Notice of Preliminary Objection dated 7/7/17. Pursuant to the application by learned Counsel to the Claimant, the said Notice of Preliminary Objection is struck out for want of prosecution.

Balogun
We have a Motion on Notice dated 31/3/17. It is brought pursuant to Order 16 Rule 1 and Order 17 Rule 1 of National Industrial Court (Civil Procedure) Rules 2017. It is for an order of Court entering final Judgment in favour of the claimant. Attached are a 7- paragraph affidavit and 10 exhibits marked Exhibit PA, A, B, C, D, E, F, G, H and I. We rely on all the averments in the affidavit. We also filed a written address dated 31/3/17. We adopt the written address as our submission and urge the Court to enter Summary Judgment in favour of the Claimant as sought

Judgment
I have proof of service of all the requisite processes on the Defendant in the Court's file. S.T. Animashahun who appeared for Defendant on 11/7/17 is aware of the

business of the day and for reason best known to him elected to stay away from proceedings of Court today.

I have read and understood all the processes filed by the Claimant for the application for Summary Judgment. I also carefully evaluated all the exhibits attached. I equally heard the oral submission of Counsel. Having done so, I find merit in the application for Summary Judgment respecting some of the claims.

Final Judgment is here entered in favour of the claimant/Applicant respecting Relief 1, 2 and 5(a) as contained in the General Form of Complaint. For the avoidance of doubt.

1. Defendant is Ordered to pay the sum of US$25,000.00 or the Naira equivalent thereto at the current CBN exchange rate to the Claimant being the total amount due to the Claimant a 2 months salary payment in lieu of termination of employment.

2. The Defendant is Ordered to pay to the Claimant the sum of $7,083.00 or the CBN current Naira equivalent thereto, being the 17days outstanding leave days accrued and unpaid for by the Defendant.

3. The Defendant is Ordered to pay the costs of flight ticket from Lagos Nigeria to Mumbai, India in the sum of N=68,900.00 to the Defendant.

All the terms of this Summary Judgment are to be complied with within 30 days from today.

Judgment is entered accordingly.

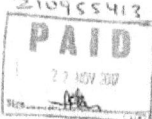

210955413

PAID

2 2 NOV 2017

Sign......

Hon. Justice J.D Peters
Presiding Judge

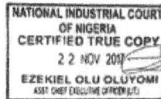

NATIONAL INDUSTRIAL COURT
OF NIGERIA
CERTIFIED TRUE COPY
2 2 NOV 201
EZEKIEL OLU OLUYOMI
ASST CHIEF EXECUTIVE OFFICER (LIT)

NATIONAL INDUSTRIAL COURT
OF NIGERIA
CERTIFIED TRUE COPY
2 2 NOV 201
EZEKIEL OLU OLUYOMI
ASST CHIEF EXECUTIVE OFFICER (LIT)

2

IN THE NATIONAL INDUSTRIAL COURT OF NIGERIA
IN THE LAGOS JUDICIAL DIVISION
HOLDEN AT LAGOS

BEFORE HIS LORDSHIP HON. JUSTICE J.D. PETERS

DATE: MONDAY 23RD OCTOBER, 2017.   SUIT NO. NICN/LA/163/2017

Between

MR. NAVEEN SHARMA   Claimant

And
GLOBACOM LIMITED   Defendant

Appearances
Claimant Attorney Present
Defendant absent

Olawale Balogun for the Claimant

Balogun
We have a pending Motion on Notice dated and filed 31/3/17. It has been served. It is for an Order of Court for Summary Judgment as contained in the Complaint and the statement of facts. It is supported by affidavit of 7 paragraphs. Attached are 10 exhibits marked as Exhibit PA, A, B, C, D, E, F, G, K and L. We rely on all the averments in the affidavit as well as the exhibits. We filed a written address of the same date. We urge the Court to grant the prayers as stated on the face of the Motion papers.

Judgment
On 11/7/17 when this matter last came up Defendant was represented by S.T. Animashahun. Today both Defendant and Counsel are not in Court. There is no reason offered for their absence.
I have read and understood all the processes filed for the application for Summary Judgment. Despite proof of service, Defendant has neither entered an appearance nor filed any defence process or even a reaction to the motion for Summary Judgment. Having listened to learned Counsel for the Applicant, I find merit in this application respecting some of the reliefs sought as follows:

1. Defendant is here ordered to pay to the Claimant/ Applicant the sum of US$20,000 or the Naira equivalent thereto at the CBN exchange rate being the total amount due to the Claimant as 2 months salary in lieu of notice of termination of employment

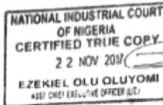

NATIONAL INDUSTRIAL COURT OF NIGERIA
CERTIFIED TRUE COPY
2 2 NOV 2017
EZEKIEL OLU OLUYOMI

Scanned by CamScanner

62

2. Defendant is ordered to pay to the Claimant/Applicant the sum of $7,667.00 of the CBN current Naira equivalent thereto being the payment for 23 days outstanding leave days accrued and unpaid for by Defendant.

3. Defendant is ordered to pay to the claimant cost of flight ticket from Lagos Nigeria to Chandigarh, India in the Sum of 47,000 Indian Rupees to the paid in Naira at the current rate of the CBN.

All the terms of this Judgment are to be complied with within 30 days from today.

Case is adjourned to 5/2/18 for the claimant to prove his Relief 3, 4, 5(b), 6 and 7. Hearing notice is to issue and be served on the Defendant with proof of same in the file.

Hon. Justice J.D Peters
Presiding Judge

NATIONAL INDUSTRIAL COURT
OF NIGERIA
CERTIFIED TRUE COPY
2 2 NOV 201
EZEKIEL OLU OLUYOMI
ASST CHIEF EXECUTIVE OFFICER (L/L)

210955412
PAID
2 2 NOV 201

Giving his view on the issue, Nigerian commercial lawyer Ovie Oddiri remarked:

"Employment contracts are sacrosanct and provide a foundation for a positive working relationship between an employee and an employer. Once an employee has carried out his duties according to the contract in a satisfactory and timely manner, he/she is entitled to their wages and it behoves on an employer to fulfill that part of the contract. This is covered by numerous case laws and statue in Nigeria.

An employee should not have to pursue their employer for payment of wages through the court systems or other non-official channels.

These allegations leveled against Globacom, the second largest telecommunications company in Nigeria, are serious and must be addressed in a proper and timely manner. We cannot to hope to attract the best skilled men and women and foreign investment and have such a stigma attached to our names."

Post-Credit Sequence

I have spoken to numerous sources who claim that mistreatment of Indian expatriate workers at Glo is a common, ongoing occurrence dating back to the noughties.

Indian PM Narendra Modi is pursuing an 'India First' policy doctrine that seeks to project Indian power internationally and consolidate Indian wealth and pride at home. Mistreatment of Indians outside the country is a highly emotive and politically charged topic in India.

There are currently more than 135 Indian-owned companies operating in Nigeria, some of which include systemically important businesses in fields like pharmaceuticals, Power and Transmission, Retail, FMCG, Automotive, Heavy Industry and Aviation.

India is now the largest buyer of Nigerian crude oil, effectively making it a systemically important foreign partner with vast influence over the economy, as Nigeria's government remains the largest source of liquidity in the economy.

Nigeria and India share a bilateral trading relationship worth $12 billion annually. A single negative change in its Nigeria policy by Narendra Modi's inward-focused current administration could significantly imperil Nigeria's economy by decimating already anaemic government revenues from crude oil sales, halting inward investment, destroying jobs and dramatically accelerating capital flight.

I reached out to Globacom to get their comment on this story, but as at press time I had received no response.

The Empire Strikes Back: Indian Workers Insist Glo is Doing Everything to Avoid Paying Them

Last month, **NewsWireNGR** published an exclusive story looking into Nigeria's second largest telecoms company's dealings with expatriate Indian labour involving allegations of unpaid entitlements, and allegedly breaking Indian employment law to carry out illegal recruitment.

Following the story, it then emerged that the expatriates in question subsequently received telephone calls from Globacom regarding their owed entitlements, which on the surface may have sounded like good news. Now however, **NewsWireNGR** can reveal what actually transpired following the story.

Blocked Websites and Incomplete Paychecks

Something that quickly emerged in the immediate aftermath of the initial story was that www.newswirengr. com was unable to load using the Glo network. A conversation with **NewsWireNGR**'s technical staff revealed that this was a technical glitch that may not necessarily have meant that Glo itself was deliberately blocking the website. However even at press time, two months later the glitch remains unresolved.

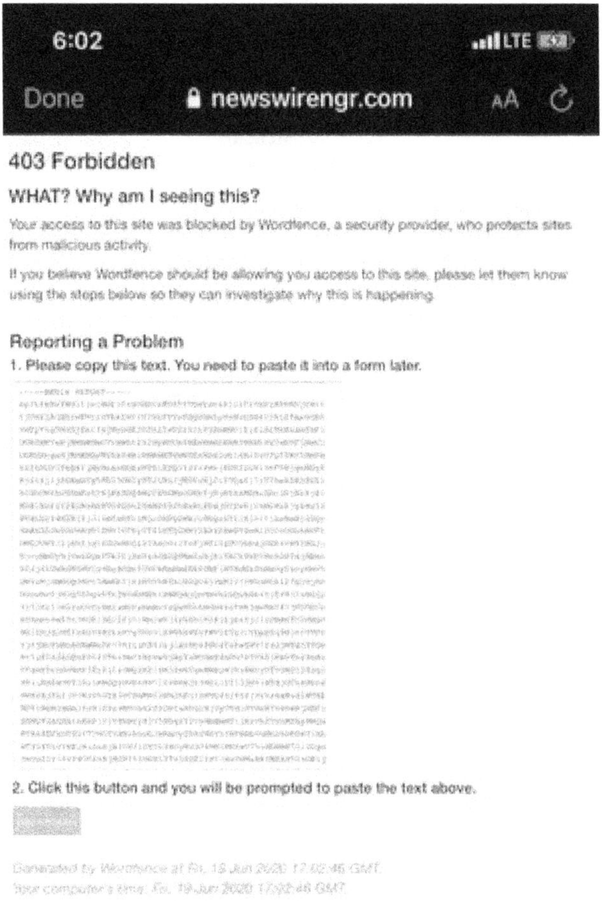

403 Forbidden

WHAT? Why am I seeing this?

Your access to this site was blocked by Wordfence, a security provider, who protects sites from malicious activity.

If you believe Wordfence should be allowing you access to this site, please let them know using the steps below so they can investigate why this is happening.

Reporting a Problem

1. Please copy this text. You need to paste it into a form later.

- - - -BEGIN REPORT- - - -
[illegible base64-like text block]

2. Click this button and you will be prompted to paste the text above.

Generated by Wordfence at Fri, 19 Jun 2020 17:02:46 GMT.
Your computer's time: Fri, 19 Jun 2020 17:02:46 GMT.

The **NewsWireNGR** website also came under fierce attack from DDOS and brute force hackers looking to bring it down. There is of course no evidence that Glo was directly linked to these events so it can perhaps be chalked up to coincidence.

All of this however pales into insignificance compared to what else happened in the immediate aftermath of the story.

According to a source who pleaded anonymity, Glo Chairman, Mike Adenuga was said to be furious about the story, though at press time, it remains to be seen what impact this will have on the aggrieved workers receiving their pay.

According to the source, the company then started calling the affected employees and offering them 1 month salary in a ratio of 60:40 (USD:NGN). It will be recalled that the entitlements owed include both the 2 months notice period and their accumulated leave allowances.

Furthermore, according to the source, Glo offered a scarcely believable NGN-USD exchange rate of N170-$1 to make the said partial payment. For reference, the current CBN rate is N385-$1 and the parallel market rate is as much as N470-$1. Unsurprisingly, this offer was unanimously rejected out of hand. Even more amazingly, the offer from Glo came with a requirement to sign and return the indemnity letter below, effectively giving up any right to ask for the rest of their entitlements or talk about the matter again.

TO: GLOBACOM LIMITED

LETTER OF RELEASE AND DISCHARGE

In consideration of the sum of $██████████████████████████ █████████, of which 60% is payable in dollars to my designated off shore account and 40% payable in naira to my account in Nigeria, offered by Globacom Limited as my full terminal entitlement and accepted by me, I, Ashiskumar Sharma of ··· ·· release and discharge Globacom Limited, its successors, subsidiaries, nominees, associates, employees, officers, agents and directors (hereinafter referred to as "the Company") for all claims, liabilities, demands, and causes of action known or unknown, fixed or contingent, which I may have or claim to have against the Company as a result of my employment in the Company from ████████20██ to the date of termination of my appointment on ████████, 20██ and do hereby agree not to file a lawsuit to assert such claims.
This includes but is not limited to claims arising under my terms and conditions of employment.

I hereby instruct the Company to remit the 60% dollar portion to my dollar account no. ·········· ······ with ·····················Bank and the 40% naira portion to my account in Nigeria, subject to applicable lawful taxes and deductions. I agree with the Company that such payments into my accounts shall be deemed to have been effected on the date of remittance, which evidence and confirmation by Company shall be conclusive.

I hereby release, waive and discharge the Company and covenant not to sue the Company for any and all liability, claims, demands, actions and causes of action whatsoever arising out of or in relation to any loss, damage or injury that may have been sustained by me, and I hereby agree to indemnify and hold harmless the Company from any losses, claims, damages, liabilities, costs and expenses (including legal fees) that it may suffer or incur arising out of or in relation to, directly or indirectly, to the subject matter of this agreement.

By this Agreement I have given the Company a full, final and irrevocable release, discharge and forbearance, which becomes effective immediately upon remittance by the Company to my accounts.

I have carefully read and fully understand all of the provisions of this agreement and release, which sets forth the entire agreement between me and the Company, and I acknowledge that I have not relied on any representation or statement, written or oral, not set forth in this document.

Signed: ████████_____

In the presence of:

Name: _____

Signature: _____

Date: _____

Attached is a copy of the data page of my current International Passport.

The source provided these screenshots of correspondence purporting to show that the company is willing to fight dirty to get out of paying them.

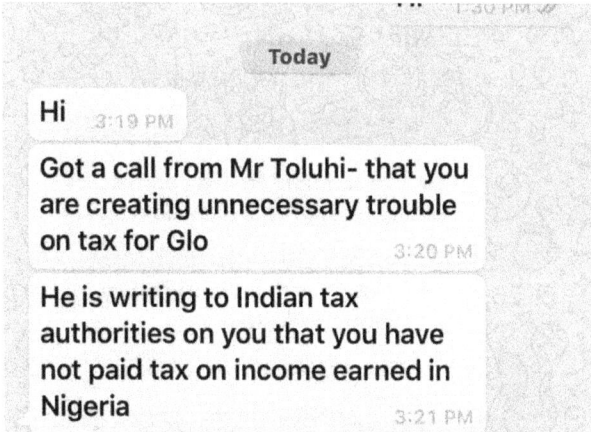

Today

Hi 3:19 PM

Got a call from Mr Toluhi- that you are creating unnecessary trouble on tax for Glo 3:20 PM

He is writing to Indian tax authorities on you that you have not paid tax on income earned in Nigeria 3:21 PM

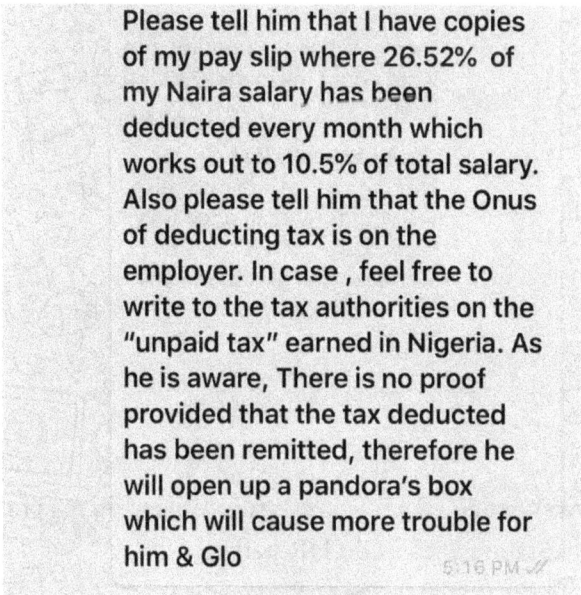

Please tell him that I have copies of my pay slip where 26.52% of my Naira salary has been deducted every month which works out to 10.5% of total salary. Also please tell him that the Onus of deducting tax is on the employer. In case , feel free to write to the tax authorities on the "unpaid tax" earned in Nigeria. As he is aware, There is no proof provided that the tax deducted has been remitted, therefore he will open up a pandora's box which will cause more trouble for him & Glo 5:16 PM

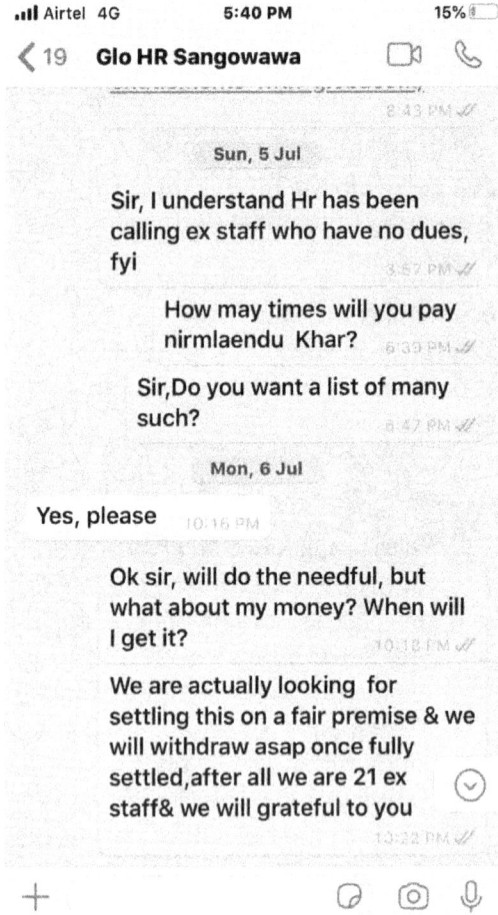

One of the affected ex-employees also provided **NewsWireNGR** with a secret recording of his telephone conversation with a Glo HR staffer.

Circumventing Indian Recruitment Laws. Again.

In the initial story, **NewsWireNGR** reported that Glo recruitment staff were apprehended by police in Mumbai and Delhi, after which they were made to leave the country. According to the source however, even this was not enough to stop Globacom from violating Indian labour regulations.

He claims that following the ban on recruiting in India, Glo now recruits prospective candidates from India, Pakistan, Egypt and elsewhere in Dubai. Prospective Indian candidates are made to fly out to the UAE where Indian police have no jurisdiction.

Just like the last time the source says, the tag team of Tony Ighalo and Adewale Sangowawa are running the Dubai operation. To get around any possible problems, candidates allegedly receive offers in the name of Conoil, Julius Berger Nigeria PLC, Abumet Nigeria Limited – a subsidiary of Julius Berger – and one 'Cobblestone Properties.'

According to him, so-called STR (Subject to Regularization) Nigerian work visas are then issued to Indian and other candidates using the above-mentioned companies, before the visas are changed on arrival in Nigeria to 'Globacom.'

Summing up his individual experience, the source said:

"Their modus operandi is to delay payments and

settlements for a year and beyond, then they call on the phone and offer one month salary. If you accept, then they send an indemnity letter and deduct 10% from the total dollar salary. They pay the balance in 60:40 dollar to naira ratio using a N170 to $1 rate while the current conversion rate is N389 to $1. The officials involved in the decision making are Sangowawa Adewale (HR) Jumoke Aduwo (HR) Gladys Talabi (Legal) & Olabisi kolesho (Deputy COO.)"

NewsWireNGR reached out to Globacom for a statement on these allegations and we will update the story as more details emerge.

V

ALLEGED FRAUD, AND DISAPPEARING ACTS: THE INSIDE STORY OF TONY DARA

In 2012, a television station widely billed as "Nigeria's answer to CNN" disappeared abruptly off the face of the earth. There was no explanation offered to anyone or any apology for disrupted services. There was especially no attempt by the station's management to account for what led to the collapse of NN24 barely two years after taking off in a blaze of publicity. All that happened in fact, was a staff exodus after being owed their wages for several months, and a quiet Facebook note from Multichoice Africa informing subscribers that the channel was being terminated.

MultiChoice Africa: Termination of NN24 and EWTN

August 23, 2012 at 5:48 PM

MultiChoice Nigeria wishes to advise DStv subscribers that NN24 (channel 414) and EWTN (channel 348) will be terminating on August 22 and August 31 respectively on the E36B (W7) platform.

MultiChoice considers a number of key factors when assessing the viability of a channel on the platform; these include the cost of distribution, the channel offering within the context of similar channels in that genre, subscriber feedback and the number of viewers and popularity of that channel.

MultiChoice Africa has reached a mutual agreement with the various channel distributors to terminate NN24 and EWTN on the W7 platform.

2   69 Comments 3 Shares

Eight years later, a similar scenario is underway at a similarly ambitious television station located approximately 26KM southeast of NN24's erstwhile Oregun, Lagos location. The story is almost exactly the same, save for the swanky location on Adeola Odeku Street, Victoria Island. Once again, it is a TV station that beats the drum about putting genuine African stories on the 24-hour global news cycle. Once again, no expenses were spared in equipping the station and building staff capacity. Once again, staff at the television station suddenly found themselves being owed up to 6 months of unpaid wages, with no explanation or resolution forthcoming from management.

Once again, there is a quiet staff exodus underway. Incredibly, some of the staff in question are also veterans of the NN24 collapse, but that is not the real story. The real story is that the person behind the meteoric rise and fall of NN24 is the same person behind the ongoing saga. His name is Anthony Dara, but everyone in the industry knows him as Tony Dara.

8 years ago under his leadership as CEO, NN24 became perhaps the highest profile Nigerian TV collapse of the decade, rivalled only by that of HiTV. This time also under his leadership as CEO, it is News Central TV that is hearing the death knell barely two years after commencing operations.

This started as a simple story about poor corporate governance and a deadbeat CEO, but it very quickly widened into a rabbit hole that included everything from institutionalised embezzlement to fund ostentatious lifestyles, to a boardroom civil war and News Central's documented business relationship with a convicted money launderer.

Tony Dara and Television: A Fractious Love Story

Prior to becoming a high profile TV executive, life was very different for Dara. In his previous life, he was a solid and unspectacular mid-level technical professional in the media space. He obtained his OND and HND in Electrical Engineering at Kaduna Polytechnic between 1992 and 1997. This was followed by a BSc in Broadcast Technology at De Montfort University in Leicester, UK at the turn of the millennium, and training at the BBC Training & Development Centre in Worcestershire, UK,

He cut his broadcasting teeth as a Technical Officer at the Nigeria Television Authority (NTA) before moving to the UK where he worked in mid-level technical roles at ITV, Bloomberg TV and Snell & Wilcox. There was nothing on this boring and competent CV to suggest that he would someday become the Bernie Madoff of Nigeria's media space, selling nonexistent dreams to investors and employees while living it up on other people's money at his $1 million Eko Pearl Tower residence.

In 2008, everything changed when he founded Nigeria's first 24-hour news channel – the West African answer to CNN as it was constantly branded. From the outset, Network News 24 (NN24) made no attempt to mask its huge ambitions, splashing out on recruitment and training of the very best new broadcasting talent in Nigeria. The company hired several eye wateringly expensive expatriate trainers and even signed an exclusive partnership with CNN in pursuit of a vision of dominating the Nigerian television news landscape.

The list of broadcasting and production talent to have passed through NN24's industry-leading training processes reads like a Who's Who of Nigerian broadcast royalty: Politics Today host, Seun Okinbaloye, TVC news anchor, Fadesola Sotinwa, Channels TV news presenter Milliscent Nnwoka, Channels TV producer Dare Idowu – the list goes on and on. It occurred to me while researching this story that nobody ever seemed to ask exactly where a TV startup obtained the money for such a huge investment from, so I pulled up NN24's CAC registration records to make sense of it.

NN24 LIMITED

NN24 LIMITED was incorporated in ABUJA, Nigeria with Registration Number 688812. It was registered on 23 Apr 2007 and it's current status is unknown. Company's registered office address is FLAT1, BLOCKD43, ZONEE8E8,EXTENSIONAPO, ABUJA, FCT

ⓘ Basic Info

Name	NN24 LIMITED
Status	Unknown
Type of Entity	Private Limited Company
Activity	UNSPECIFIED
Registration Number	RC 688812
Registration Date	23 Apr 2007

♀ Registered Address

Address	FLAT1, BLOCKD43, ZONEE8E8,EXTENSIONAPO, ABUJA, FCT
State	FCT
LGA	
City	ABUJA
Phone number	
Website, Email	

👥 Owners / Directors / Key management personal

Name	Designation
Mustapha Bintu Dido	Director

Name	Designation
Dr. Rauligun Emmanuel	Director
Team Kenneth	Director
Abari Terungwa	Director
Egwu Samuel Odouyi	Director
Audu-naslgbe Meta	Director
Dr. Nuhu Shem Zagbayi	Director
Mustapha Bela Lido	Director
Dr. Bologun Elnhanuel	Director
Team Kenneth	Director
Dr. Nuhu Shem Zagbayi	Director
Anthony Bara	Director
Gabriel Tanimu Aduda	Director
Abari Terungwa	Director
Egwu Samuel Odoiyoi	Director
Audu-ronigbe Metu	Director

Additional info

Branch address

Head office address

Objectives

The first name on the list of directors should provide an insight into the calibre of people that Dara has access to in Nigeria. Boss Gidahyelda Mustapha is Nigeria's current Secretary to the Government of the Federation (SGF), and one of the most powerful people in Abuja. As far back as 2007 when NN24 was registered, Dara had access to Mustapha, who was then a member of Interim Management Committee of the defunct Petroleum (Special) Trust Fund (PTF), along with other recognisable names on the list of directors like Philips Tanimu Aduda, who was then a House of Representatives member and is currently a Senator representing the FCT.

It is important to keep this in mind because as this story progresses, it becomes clear that such access is central to the Tony Dara myth. Bear in mind that the average annual wage for a broadcast engineer in London is currently £41,002 according to Glassdoor. Adjusted for inflation, he was making roughly £31,200/year in 2005 money – hardly a king's ransom and certainly not enough to set up an expensive 24-hour news channel affiliated with CNN. So what was his deal?

The Tony Dara Formula

I spoke to six different whistleblowers who are current and ex-staff of News Central TV, and from their different accounts, three common denominators came through. First that Dara is a malignant narcissist who sees everyone else as a supporting character in his own personal lifetime videogame – hence his ability to owe people indefinitely without a shred of remorse; second that he lives a wildly ostentatious lifestyle that his actual legitimate income cannot possibly support; and third that he is a consummate liar who habitually feeds porkies to everyone including employees and investors.

A former News Central staff member described him to me as "someone who tries to live a lifestyle to give the impression that he is some sort of media mogul." Staff at News Central are typically given the impression that he owns at least a stake in the company, and they are constantly reassured that "money is not a problem" due to the presence of a mystery investor with very deep pockets. That notwithstanding, everyone I spoke to complained that since January this year, payment of salaries has happened only once, something that is confirmed by company internal communication embedded below.

[Ncstaff] Recommencement of News Central Digital
1 message

Tolu Oladipo <tolu.oladipo@newscentral.ng>
To: ncstaff@newscentral.ng

Fri, May 1, 2020 at 12:12

Dear Colleagues,

The last few weeks and months have indeed been unusual. In addition to the business headwinds we faced as a startup, the shutdown and restrictions on movement in response to the COVID-19 pandemic added significantly to the challenging business environment. We want to salute the patience and resilience of the entire News Central family and encourage our colleagues to remain resolute and optimistic despite the constant barrage of negative news and depressing statistics.

As you are aware, the Federal Government of Nigeria has announced gradual easing of the lockdown starting on Monday May4, 2020. As such, News Central will be reactivating business activities also in a phased manner, commencing with our Digital platforms. The commencement of business activities will incorporate significant remote working initiatives and will be in compliance with public health protocols at all times as relates to the COVID-19 pandemic.

In light of this you are all requested to note the following:

1. *Staff will be paid outstanding salaries up to March 31, 2020 and this will be released as the funds become available. As communicated previously, leave without pay remains in place from April 1, 2020 unless otherwise advised*
2. *Members of the team will be recalled from leave on an individual basis and will be advised of their updated duties and whether to work remotely or on-site*
3. *On-site work on the office premises will be subject to the following guidelines:*
4.   a. *Handwashing and/or hand sanitizing will be required before gaining access to the premises*
      b. *Facemasks will be mandatory within the office for all occupants at all times until studio broadcasts resume*
      c. *Social distancing protocols will require seating of only one person per desk at any given time*
      d. *Staff who feel unwell should either remain at home or leave the office premises immediately and report their symptoms to their line supervisor*
5. *Policy guidelines for remote work will be circulated once approved, and will replace the current policy in the handbook*

Based on the foregoing, work has commenced to enable the resumption of content on our Digital platforms starting May 4, 2020. In light of this, team members required to actualize this will be contacted directly and briefed from today.

It is our strong belief that we have overcome the most trying period of our corporate existence since inception and this marks the return of the project back to its stated objectives. We believe the worst is over and we want to thank you all for your continued patience and maturity during this period.

Best regards,

THE JUNGLE

Tolu Oladipo
Head Human Resources

cid:image001.png@01D43ED7.AE86FD40

Website: www.newscentral.ng **Tel:** +234 803 344 1586
Nigeria Office: The Post Square Building, Adeola Odeku
Victoria Island, Lagos, Nigeria

icon_0004_icons-01 bar1 icon_0003_icons-02 bar1 icon_0002_icons-03 bar1 icon_0001_icons-04 bar1 icon_0000_icons-05

Virus-free. www.avg.com

M

[Ncstaff] Unpaid Salaries
1 message

NC Non-core Team <ncnoncoreteam@gmail.com>   Wed, Mar 25, 2020 at 11:40
To: Tony.dara@newscentral.ng, Tonydara@me.com
Cc: ncstaff@newscentral.ng

Dear Tony

Trust this email finds you well.

You will recall on March 16th you met with two representatives of non-core team staff members of News Central in your office in the presence of Mr. Tayo Ojeleke, the company secretary. The meeting was to resolve issues regarding outstanding salaries of NC employees. The resolution of that meeting was a verbal commitment from you to resolve payment of outstanding salaries on or before the expiration of 72 hours (effectively COB Thursday 19th March 2020).

Evidently, at the time of this email, you have again failed to honour your obligation without further or information or explanation.

As a result of this disposition, we believe the current situation regarding unpaid salaries since January 2020 and your failure to provide reasonable communication on the matter has gone beyond reproach to downright demeaning and disrespect.

It is important you understand in unambiguous terms the varied difficulties this situation has put many of us through. Many families are stranded and unable to pay bills. Majority of us now have unpaid loans. It is equally important for you to be aware there are those who are terribly sick or ailing or with underlying medical issues and unable to seek and pay for medicals due to our inability to access the company's healthcare/HMO scheme which was suspended.

The current coronavirus pandemic means our very lives and those of our families are further exposed to avoidable danger without the financial resources to respond adequately as a result of non payment of salaries.

As a team of dedicated and professional staff, we have demonstrated commitment to our work since the inception of the company. Our loyalty to the vision of a Pan African 24-hour station still remains resolute. We have also displayed exemplary patience and understanding during times of challenges. We appreciate the nature of the business as a start-up and expect there will be teething problems.

However, the inability of NC to pay staff salaries is fast approaching the third month despite having received several promises from you on salaries and other deliverables as the CEO; majority of which, if not ALL, have failed to materialize.

It has now become increasingly difficult if not impossible to rely on your word as the Managing Director and CEO. This will no doubt affect our ability to trust the leadership of the company in terms of steering it's affairs if and when we resume following the resolution of this matter.

Like you stated in a Whatsapp message sent on March 3rd, you and you alone must take "full responsibility of the situation as the leader of the team and MD/CEO of the company".

The logical conclusion is that it has now become extremely difficult and frankly a bit too much to ask staff to keep trusting our interests are being considered at all by you. We signed up to work for a company and our engagement was backed up with a contract of employment, which the company under you, has defaulted on with impunity.

To this effect, we formally demand the payment of all outstanding salaries on or before Tuesday 31st March, 2020. Failure do to so will leave us with no option than to seek redress from the appropriate quarters.

We hope as CEO you will do the needful within the stipulated time in the interest of the company.

Regards
Non-core team staff

THE JUNGLE

[Ncstaff] Unpaid Salaries
1 message

NC Non-core Team <ncnoncoreteam@gmail.com>   Wed, Mar 25, 2020 at 11:40
To: Tony dara@newscentral.ng, Tonydara@me.com
Cc: ncstaff@newscentral.ng

Dear Tony

Trust this email finds you well.

You will recall on March 16th you met with two representatives of non-core team staff members of News Central in your office in the presence of Mr. Tayo Ojeleke, the company secretary. The meeting was to resolve issues regarding outstanding salaries of NC employees. The resolution of that meeting was a verbal commitment from you to resolve payment of outstanding salaries on or before the expiration of 72 hours (effectively COB Thursday 19th March 2020).

Evidently, at the time of this email, you have again failed to honour your obligation without further or information or explanation.

As a result of this disposition, we believe the current situation regarding unpaid salaries since January 2020 and your failure to provide reasonable communication on the matter has gone beyond reproach to downright demeaning and disrespect.

It is important you understand in unambiguous terms the varied difficulties this situation has put many of us through. Many families are stranded and unable to pay bills. Majority of us now have unpaid loans. It is equally important for you to be aware there are those who are terribly sick or ailing or with underlying medical issues and unable to seek and pay for medicals due to our inability to access the company's healthcare/HMO scheme which was suspended.

The current coronavirus pandemic means our very lives and those of our families are further exposed to avoidable danger without the financial resources to respond adequately as a result of non payment of salaries.

As a team of dedicated and professional staff, we have demonstrated commitment to our work since the inception of the company. Our loyalty to the vision of a Pan African 24-hour station still remains resolute. We have also displayed exemplary patience and understanding during times of challenges. We appreciate the nature of the business as a start-up and expect there will be teething problems.

However, the inability of NC to pay staff salaries is fast approaching the third month despite having received several promises from you on salaries and other deliverables as the CEO; majority of which, if not ALL, have failed to materialize.

It has now become increasingly difficult if not impossible to rely on your word as the Managing Director and CEO. This will no doubt affect our ability to trust the leadership of the company in terms of steering it's affairs if and when we resume following the resolution of this matter.

Like you stated in a Whatsapp message sent on March 3rd, you and you alone must take "full responsibility of the situation as the leader of the team and MD/CEO of the company."

The logical conclusion is that it has now become extremely difficult and frankly a bit too much to ask staff to keep trusting our interests are being considered at all by you. We signed up to work for a company and our engagement was backed up with a contract of employment, which the company under you, has defaulted on with impunity.

To this effect, we formally demand the payment of all outstanding salaries on or before Tuesday 31st March, 2020. Failure do to so will leave us with no option than to seek redress from the appropriate quarters.

We hope as CEO you will do the needful within the stipulated time in the interest of the company.

Regards
Non-core team staff

85

[Ncstaff] Unpaid Salaries

1 message

NC Non-core Team <ncnoncoreteam@gmail.com>   Wed, Mar 25, 2020 at 11:40
To: Tony.dara@newscentral.ng, Tonydara@me.com
Cc: ncstaff@newscentral.ng

Dear Tony

Trust this email finds you well.

You will recall on March 16th you met with two representatives of non-core team staff members of News Central in your office in the presence of Mr. Tayo Ojeleke, the company secretary. The meeting was to resolve issues regarding outstanding salaries of NC employees. The resolution of that meeting was a verbal commitment from you to resolve payment of outstanding salaries on or before the expiration of 72 hours (effectively COB Thursday 19th March 2020).

Evidently, at the time of this email, you have again failed to honour your obligation without further or information or explanation.

As a result of this disposition, we believe the current situation regarding unpaid salaries since January 2020 and your failure to provide reasonable communication on the matter has gone beyond reproach to downright demeaning and disrespect.

It is important you understand in unambiguous terms the varied difficulties this situation has put many of us through. Many families are stranded and unable to pay bills. Majority of us now have unpaid loans. It is equally important for you to be aware there are those who are terribly sick or ailing or with underlying medical issues and unable to seek and pay for medicals due to our inability to access the company's healthcare/HMO scheme which was suspended.

The current coronavirus pandemic means our very lives and those of our families are further exposed to avoidable danger without the financial resources to respond adequately as a result of non payment of salaries.

As a team of dedicated and professional staff, we have demonstrated commitment to our work since the inception of the company. Our loyalty to the vision of a Pan African 24-hour station still remains resolute. We have also displayed exemplary patience and understanding during times of challenges. We appreciate the nature of the business as a start-up and expect there will be teething problems.

However, the inability of NC to pay staff salaries is fast approaching the third month despite having received several promises from you on salaries and other deliverables as the CEO, majority of which, if not ALL, have failed to materialize.

It has now become increasingly difficult if not impossible to rely on your word as the Managing Director and CEO. This will no doubt affect our ability to trust the leadership of the company in terms of steering it's affairs if and when we resume following the resolution of this matter.

Like you stated in a Whatsapp message sent on March 3rd, you and you alone must take 'full responsibility of the situation as the leader of the team and MD/CEO of the company'

The logical conclusion is that it has now become extremely difficult and frankly a bit too much to ask staff to keep trusting our interests are being considered at all by you. We signed up to work for a company and our engagement was backed up with a contract of employment, which the company under you, has defaulted on with impunity.

To this effect, we formally demand the payment of all outstanding salaries on or before Tuesday 31st March, 2020. Failure do to so will leave us with no option than to seek redress from the appropriate quarters.

We hope as CEO you will do the needful within the stipulated time in the interest of the company.

Regards
Non-core team staff

[Ncstaff] Unpaid Salaries
1 message

NC Non-core Team <ncnoncoreteam@gmail.com>   Mon, Apr 20, 2020 at 10:13
To: Tony.dara@newscentral.ng, Tonydara@me.com
Cc: ncstaff@newscentral.ng

Dear Mr Dara,

Given the situation with the Covid-19 pandemic, we hope you and your loved ones are safe and this email meets you well.

That being said, we once again write to you as the CEO, in respect to outstanding salaries owed to staff by News Central TV.

Like many businesses there will be challenges with regards to securing funding, and you have on a few occasions informed us of ongoing efforts on your part to secure additional investment funds.

Following our email to you on 25th March, DEMANDING the payment of ALL outstanding salaries; we received only 50% payment for that of January 2020 made to staff on Friday 27th March. Other emails have been silent on providing a specific date as to when the balance would be paid.

Also there have been no further communication articulating a cogent and compelling business plan for the future of the company.

Consequently, we are left with no alternate but to once more demand all outstanding salaries for the remainder of January, as well as those for February - March, 2020.

As seen with the communication from the HR on 25th March, stating that all staff will be paid outstanding salaries, also going further to point out that all staff are "to proceed on leave without pay from April 1, 2020."

This was not only insensitive of News Central but has heightened the uncertainty about the future of the company as a growing concern.

So whilst this 'compulsory leave' is being observed, we are yet to receive the promised payments, and as has often been the practice with your management team, no further communication has been made.

It is important to remind you of the obvious dire circumstances which majority if not all staff are forced to contend with on a daily basis following the Covid-19 pandemic. Our financial position in a very uncertain world has been made more severe due to the delays in the said payment.

The lack of empathy and due consideration for the plight of staff can only mean our sufferings have been lost to what we hoped would be your good conscience.

It is now clear that you have treated and continue to treat such serious matters with levity and consequently, chosen to sacrifice careers and reputations including yours, on the altar of a dysfunctional leadership style; and have failed to understand it can no longer be business as usual.

To this end, the non-core team staff make this FINAL DEMAND by insisting on payment of our outstanding salaries and other benefits as per our contract of employment within the next 14 days, otherwise we will resort to taking appropriate steps against News Central TV.

Regards,
Non-core team staff

[Quoted text hidden]

[Ncstaff] Unpaid Salaries
1 message

NC Non-core Team <ncnoncoreteam@gmail.com>   Mon, Apr 20, 2020 at 10:13
To: Tony.dara@newscentral.ng, Tonydara@me.com
Cc: ncstaff@newscentral.ng

Dear Mr Dara,

Given the situation with the Covid-19 pandemic, we hope you and your loved ones are safe and this email meets you well.

That being said, we once again write to you as the CEO, in respect to outstanding salaries owed to staff by News Central TV.

Like many businesses there will be challenges with regards to securing funding, and you have on a few occasions informed us of ongoing efforts on your part to secure additional investment funds.

Following our email to you on 25th March, DEMANDING the payment of ALL outstanding salaries, we received only 50% payment for that of January 2020 made to staff on Friday 27th March. Other emails have been silent on providing a specific date as to when the balance would be paid.

Also there have been no further communication articulating a cogent and compelling business plan for the future of the company.

Consequently, we are left with no alternate but to once more demand all outstanding salaries for the remainder of January, as well as those for February - March, 2020.

As seen with the communication from the HR on 25th March, stating that all staff will be paid outstanding salaries, also going further to point out that all staff are "to proceed on leave without pay from April 1, 2020."

This was not only insensitive of News Central but has heightened the uncertainty about the future of the company as a growing concern.

So whilst this 'compulsory leave' is being observed, we are yet to receive the promised payments, and as has often been the practice with your management team, no further communication has been made.

It is important to remind you of the obvious dire circumstances which majority if not all staff are forced to contend with on a daily basis following the Covid-19 pandemic. Our financial position in a very uncertain world has been made more severe due to the delays in the said payment.

The lack of empathy and due consideration for the plight of staff can only mean our sufferings have been lost to what we hoped would be your good conscience.

It is now clear that you have treated and continue to treat such serious matters with levity and consequently, chosen to sacrifice careers and reputations including yours, on the altar of a dysfunctional leadership style, and have failed to understand it can no longer be business as usual.

To this end, the non-core team staff make this FINAL DEMAND by insisting on payment of our outstanding salaries and other benefits as per our contract of employment within the next 14 days, otherwise we will resort to taking appropriate steps against News Central TV.

Regards,
Non-core team staff

This is to advise you that staff pensions for the month of January 2020 have been remitted to t
staff who are yet to submit their RSA account details (or who are unsure whether they have dor
details of your pension account to Mimi for compilation. This should reach her before close of I
8, 2020. For those who do not have a pension account, you are encouraged to do so with the PI
submit the details to Mimi.

Best regards,

Tolu Oladipo

Head Human Resources

cid:image001.png@01D43ED7.AE86FD40

Website: www.newscentral.ng   **Tel:** +234 803 344 1586

Nigeria Office: The Post Square Building, Adeola Odeku

Victoria Island, Lagos, Nigeria

icon_0004_icons-01 bar1 icon_0003_icons-02 bar1 icon_0002_icons-03 bar1 icon
icon_0000_icons-05

Virus-free. www.avg.com

NATIONAL PENSION COMMISSION

Plot 174, Adetokunbo Ademola Crescent Wuse II, Abuja - Nigeria
E-mail: info@pencom.gov.ng Website: www.pencom.gov.ng
Tel: +234(9)4611454 - 59, +234 (9) 461 39 35

PENCOM/INSP/C&E/ENF/CMT/109/19/1106

05 November, 2019

The Managing Director
News Central Television
Post Square Building
Adeola Odeku Street Victoria Island
Lagos

LETTER OF CAUTION

Dear Sir,

RE: NON REMITTANCE OF PENSION CONTRIBUTIONS INTO YOUR EMPLOYEES RETIREMENT SAVINGS ACCOUNT

Please, refer to our letter of 12 September, 2019 ref: PENCOM/INSP/C&E/ENF/CMT/109/19/940 on the above subject.

The Commission is concerned about your failure to respond to our earlier letter. However, in furtherance of its philosophy of seeking Stakeholders cooperation, the Commission has granted you an additional two weeks within which to forward evidence(s) of compliance.

Please note that your continued failure to provide the required information may leave the Commission with no option but to apply appropriate sanctions including legal action against your Organisation.

Thank you

Yours faithfully,

S. M. Bwala
Head, Compliance & Enforcement Department

Page 1 of 1

Confidential

NEWS CENTRAL

MEMORANDUM

To: ALL STAFF
Cc: MD/CEO
From: HUMAN RESOURCES
Date: March 27, 2020
Subject: PAYMENT OF SALARY TRANCHE

We refer to our previous communications on salary payment. Unfortunately we are yet to receive sufficient funds to clear the arrears of salaries owed. Notwithstanding we recognize that staff have been placed under severe financial pressure which has been made worse by the restrictions arising from the COVID-19 outbreak.

To this end, a decision has been made to apply the quantum of money just received towards staff salaries. This will only cover 50% of January salaries at this time and we expect do disburse this to individual accounts starting today. We are hopeful that additional funds will be received soon, and we will continue to prioritize salary payments until the backlog is cleared and we are able to normalize operations. We request the patience and understanding of staff in this regard.

We also want to encourage staff to stay safe during this period. The financial challenges coupled with the ongoing challenges arising from the pandemic are liable to cause fear and anxiety. We strongly believe that such challenges are temporary and like all such previous challenges, we will overcome them and come out stronger on the other side. Let's keep our spirits up and take responsible health-conscious decisions during this time.

Best regards.

Tolu Oladipo
Head Human Resources

In response to all of the questions and suggestions above, the staff at News Central received no response from Dara whatsoever. According to the whistleblowers, this is classic Tony Dara – create a problem, usually financial, leave it for employees to clean up, usually by being owed indefinitely, then activate radio silence from his Pearl Tower residence, sometimes traveling abroad and going silent for weeks at a time.

My main source informed me that whereas the initial agreement with the mystery investor was that $2.5 million would cover all takeoff expenses, News Central actually spent more than $4 million and kept asking for more cash injections from the investor. Apparently tired of the rigmarole and having become distrustful of Dara, the investor then carried out an audit in November, after which he immediately switched off the cash supply going into the new year. This apparently, is the genesis of the 6-month salary backlog.

Incredibly, even amidst a salary backlog and the COVID-19 outbreak, a source who asked to remain anonymous informed me that Dara's brain was still working overtime trying to find an exploitable loophole to raid the station of its expensive equipment and thus effectively bilk the investor one last time.

This picture of Tony Dara was corroborated by every single current and past News Central employee who agreed to speak to me. Here is an interesting quote from one of them.

"What we have here is a classic case of some form of corporate mismanagement in connection with the company's operations. This has resulted in adverse effects causing serious reputation damage to the fledging brand. I would like to appeal to the Board and Management of

News Central to make payment or payment arrangement on salaries and other statutory payments the company owes its current and ex-employees as soon as possible. Months of delay and lack of effective communication in the face of a pandemic has brought untold suffering and hardship to staff. If Mr. Dara fails to do this, it is only expected the aggrieved party will look for available means to enforce their rights including taking legal action.

Most worrisome is the glaring similarities between what happened at his defunct NN24 and what is going on at News Central – Months of unpaid salaries, failure to remit Pensions and PAYE, frivolous spending of investment funds, termination of employment contracts without the means to settle the obligations etc. In the circle of life, Tony Dara has clearly demonstrated he is unable and unwilling to tame his private demons. They devoured NN24 and are circling and waiting to descend on New Central TV. He should face the fact that he has snuffed life out of the company and must realize vultures are already in the air waiting to pile in and squabble over the spoils. Unlike NN24, I am concerned for him and the company because this time around their descent will be rapid."

– Michael Smith (former Head Risk and Compliance, News Central)

The next quote came from a current staffer who

asked to remain anonymous so as not to jeopardise the slim chance of receiving his owed entitlements.

"I have not been paid since around the start of the year. My biggest problem with Tony is that he takes no responsibility. Tony's first reaction to problems is to run away. There seems to have been a falling out between the investor and Tony. I hear the investor believes that he converted over N200 million to personal use, which was why an audit was carried out in November. Following the audit, the money taps were turned off.

"Tony is into lavish living, but has not made the money to sustain this lifestyle. The other thing with Tony is that polite communication doesn't work with him. You have to drag him down 3rd Mainland Bridge by his ears. He's a narcissist like you have never seen before. He is entitled beyond the point of belief. Tony doesn't feel like he is responsible or should be questioned at all. At the moment, none of us has any work to do, we're basically just sitting around doing nothing."

– Anonymous current staffer

So Who Owns News Central? Answer: Not Tony Dara

So far, we have established that Dara's basic formula at NN24 and at News Central was to sell a dream to rich investors, and pretend to build a world class TV station with their money, only to end up deliberately running it into the ground and filling his pockets at the expense of unpaid staff. Without arriving at any specifics, the composition of the NN24 board of directors gives a rough idea about whose money Dara made away with at NN24. That leaves the question, whose money is being siphoned into Dara's pockets via News Central? Who exactly is this mystery 'investor' that my whistleblowers kept referencing?

Not even the whistleblowers knew the answer to that question, so I went digging again, expecting to find a stone-wall or a never-ending maze of holding companies and shell corporations registered in the British Virgin Islands. Short of a collaborative effort on the scale of the Panama Papers, not even I would be able to unravel such a web. Instead, what I found shocked me because, (a) it was not particularly hard to find and (b) the names in question potentially create a conflict of interest that would negate the entire premise for News Central's existence.

Amazingly for the type of people involved, these investors actually put their own names on News Central's CAC registration documents, so that when I pulled up the records, this was what I saw:

NEWS CENTRAL MEDIA LIMITED

NEWS CENTRAL MEDIA LIMITED was incorporated in LAGOS, Nigeria with Registration Number 1452929. It was registered on 09 Jul 2018 and it's current status is unknown. Company's registered office address is 23A AT MURI OKUNOLA STREET, VICTORIA ISLAND, LAGOS.

ℹ Basic Info

Name	NEWS CENTRAL MEDIA LIMITED
Status	Unknown
Type of Entity	Private Company Limited By Shares
Activity	Printing and reproduction of recorded media
Registration Number	RC 1452929
Registration Date	09 Jul 2018

📍 Registered Address

Address	23A AT MURI OKUNOLA STREET, VICTORIA ISLAND, LAGOS
State	LAGOS
LGA	ETI-OSA
City	LAGOS
Phone number	
Website email	seal_9266@hotmail.com

👥 Owners / Directors / Key management personal

Name	Designation
James Onanefe Ibori	Director

Name	Designation
Romeo Eghene	Director
Oluwatoni Aishleye Alao	Secretary
Joshua Onanefe Ibori	Shareholder
Romeo Eghene	Shareholder
Segun Osofade	Applicant

📋 Additional info

Branch address
Head office address
Objectives

🔗 Associated Searches

Name	City

💬 NEWS CENTRAL MEDIA LIMITED Reviews
No reviews

You didn't misread that!

Yes, that is the James Onanefe Ibori, ex-governor of Delta State and de-facto godfather of Delta State politics. The one who was convicted in the UK for stealing at least £50 million (N24 billion) from Delta State, and spent four years in a British prison for the offence. The one who Scotland Yard estimates stole up to £157 million (N76 billion) of public funds. Presumably, after being publicly jailed for stealing and laundering money.

The other director mentioned, Romeo Omuvwie Oghene is an interesting case study into how fronting works in the monied political circles. Apart from a nearly blank LinkedIn profile simply describing him as a "public servant," he has no significant web presence.

Romeo Oghene · 3rd   🔒 Message   More...

Public Servant at Delta State Government   Delta State Government

Nigeria · 55 connections · Contact info

Experience

Public Servant
Delta State Government
Dec 2015 – Present · 4 yrs 7 mos
Nigeria

A bit of digging however, turns up obscure reference naming him as an Executive Assistant to the Governor, Special Duties, Delta State. A bit more digging shows that in 2011, he contested as a PDP candidate in the Delta State House of Assembly election for Ethiope West.

Here it gets more interesting. In 2015, Ibori's daughter, Erhiatake Ibori also contested as a PDP candidate for the Ethiope West state assembly seat – an election that she won and openly dedicated to her "political father" Ifeanyi Okowa, who is the current governor of Delta State. Okowa by the way, is a publicly acknowledged and self-declared political godson of James Ibori. He even makes sure to publicly celebrate Ibori's birthday every year, criminal conviction or not.

Putting this puzzle together, we then have a News Central board member James Ibori, sitting alongside the other News Central board member Romeo Oghene, who just so happens to be a close associate and employee of Ibori's godson, and is also from Ibori's political constituency in Delta State. If you were a serving public official – say, a governor for example – and you do not want your name coming up on public CAC records, then what better way to mask your investment than by using a close and loyal ally as a bag carrier?

Of course without documented evidence to say so, this does not suggest that News Central is in fact partly owned by a proxy working for the current Delta State governor, but it does raise a few key issues surrounding how the CAC and NBC treats Politically Exposed Persons (PEPs) in Nigeria. If an ex-convict openly accused by a credible foreign government of stealing up to N76bn can walk into these organisations and walk out with a certificate saying that he owns a multimillion dollar TV station with no questions asked, then there is clearly a process problem. If the NBC can also look on as a TV station owes its staff even through the difficult circumstances of a lockdown without imposing sanctions, then there is also a process problem there.

Finally, if dirty money is allowed to commingle freely with legitimate investment on CAC record books, then there is no disincentive for the political class to steal public funds and use them to artificially dominate the economy.

Genuine Nigerian television startups should not be at a competitive disadvantage because they do not have $4 million to burn through before even going on air, never mind making any money. If this keeps on happening, the best Nigeria can aspire to, is an economic state similar to that of post-Soviet Russia.

The takeaways from this investigation can be summed up as follows:

1. Tony Dara is a broadcast engineer with a taste for the finer things in life who has somehow managed to convince two different sets of HNI investors that he is qualified to a 24-hour news TV station, in the process wasting millions

of dollars that go into funding his lifestyle while he runs down the station and owes staff indefinitely.

2. Convicted fraudster and money launderer James Onanefe Ibori, in partnership with at least one of his political proxies is the owner of News Central TV.

3. There appears to be no process in place to prevent a situation where a PEP such as Ibori can become the sole proprietor of an entity rendering a public interest service such as news.

4. The NBC, which is quick to hand out fines and hoard broadcast licenses for mundane reasons seems to have no problem with employees of broadcast organisations being owed their entitlements habitually.

5. Using the unfair advantage of illegally acquired funds, politicians like Ibori and the politically connected have every intention of using investment and acquisition to create a captive economy that makes fair competition impossible.

I reached out to Tony Dara for his comments on the story before going to press, but as expected there has been no reply.

Request for Comment

Add label

David Hundeyin Yesterday
to tony.dara

From   **David Hundeyin** · dihundeyin@gmail.com

To   tony.dara@newscentral.ng

Date   Jun 24, 2020, 4:47 PM

View security details

Greetings,

My name is David Hundeyin and I am an independent journalist working on a story about alleged financial mismanagement and impending total collapse at News Central under your leadership.

I would like to get your comment on this matter.

Best

↩ Reply   ↩ Reply all   ↪ Forward

In the meantime, more whistleblowers at News Central have also indicated their willingness to go on record. **NewswireNGR** will bring you further updates as the story develops.

VI

INSINCERITY, BAD FAITH AND ISOMORPHIC MIMICRY: THE HARMONISED POLICE BILL 2020 IN FOCUS

On Thursday September 17, President Muhammadu Buhari signed an important piece of legislation into law.

The new harmonised Nigeria Police Force Establishment bill was hailed by presidential Special Adviser on Media and Publicity, Femi Adesina as a modern framework that would transform the police into a "more effective and well organized Police Force, driven by the principles of transparency and accountability in its operations and management of its resources".

According to the presidency, the Act among other things, established a fit-for-purpose funding framework for the NPF to bring it in line with other key Federal institutions. It would also enhance police professionalism through increased training opportunities and create a proper template for symbiotic relations between the NPF and local communities to maintain law and order across Nigeria.

The news of the bill's signing was met with praise by several prominent individuals including the UK High Commissioner to Nigeria Catriona Laing, who described it as a "key step toward modernising" the NPF.

NewsWireNGR went through the bill to ascertain whether it was in fact what it was presented as, or yet another piece of vaguely-worded legislation that opens the door to regulatory overreach and systemic arbitrage.

Our findings once again indicated that it was very much the latter. The problems identified in new Police Act boil down to the following three issues: liberal expansion of subjective, ambiguously-worded powers of the police to stop, search and arrest Nigerians at will without any specific or enforceable limit to these subjective powers; a funding framework that effectively incentivizes and legalises shakedowns of citizens by the police; and wording that shields the police from responsibility for police misbehaviour, while effectively criminalising Nigerians for speaking out against such misbehaviour.

Sweeping, Ambiguously-Worded, Subjective Police Powers

The problems begin in Section 34 of the Bill where it states that a suspect may not be handcuffed, bound or subjected to restraint except "there is reasonable apprehension of violence or an attempt to escape."

34. A suspect or defendant may not be handcuffed, bound or subjected to restraint except:

    (a) there is reasonable apprehension of violence or an attempt to escape;

    (b) the restraint is considered necessary for the safety of the suspect or defendant; or

    (c) by order of a court.

In practice, this innocent-looking clause means that whenever a Nigerian has an encounter with the police, the only limiting factor stopping them from being treated like a convict is the individual subjective opinion of the officer in charge. If the officer woke up on the wrong side of the bed and he/she decides that they suspect a Nigerian of potential violence, they can restrain them in the typical manner of the Nigerian police. It is important to note why this point is so important because it sets the tone for a lot of how the rest of the bill is framed.

According to SBM Intelligence co-founder Cheta Nwanze, the insertion of vague or unenforceable clauses in Nigerian legislation is typically an attempt to confer subjectively and selectively enforceable power on the Nigerian state. In other words, when drafting a bill in Nigeria that involves interaction between the state and the public, the extent of the state's powers must be very clearly and objectively defined, with as little room for subjective interpretations as possible.

Section 38 effectively ends the right to assumed innocence which is one of the founding principles of the 1999 constitution.

38.   (1) A police officer may, without an order of a court and without a warrant, arrest a suspect:

(a) whom he suspects on reasonable grounds of having committed an offence against a law in Nigeria or against the law of any other country, unless the law creating the offence provides that the suspect cannot be arrested without a warrant;

(b) who commits any offence in his presence;

(c) who obstructs a police officer while in the execution of his duty, or who has escaped or attempts to escape from lawful custody;

(d) in whose possession anything is found which may reasonably be suspected to be stolen property or who may reasonably be suspected of having committed an offence with reference to the thing;

(e) whom he suspects on reasonable grounds of being a deserter from any of the armed forces of Nigeria;

(f) whom he suspects on reasonable grounds of having been involved in an act committed at a place outside Nigeria which, if committed in Nigeria, would have been punished as an offence, and for which he is, under a law in force in Nigeria, liable to be apprehended and detained in Nigeria;

(g) having in his possession without lawful excuse, the burden of proving which excuse shall lie on the person, any implement of housebreaking, car theft, firearm or any offensive or dangerous weapon;

(h) whom he has reasonable cause to believe a warrant of arrest has been issued by a court of competent jurisdiction in Nigeria;

(i) found in Nigeria taking precautions to conceal his presence in circumstances, which afford reason to believe that he is taking such precautions with a view to committing an offence;

(j) whom he is directed to arrest by a Judge or magistrate.

(k) whom he reasonably suspects to be planning to commit an offence for which the police officer may arrest without a warrant, if it appears to him that the commission of the offence cannot be otherwise prevented; or

It empowers any police officer without the authority of a court order or a warrant to arrest anyone "whom he suspects on reasonable grounds of having committed an offense against a law in Nigeria, or against the law of any other country." Sub-section D of this utterly nonsensical section also gives the police the power to arrest anyone based on their subjective idea of whether they think an item in that person's possession may have been stolen.

Once again without recourse to a court order or a warrant, a police officer can decide to stop a young man with an iPhone X, accuse said young man of having 'stolen' it based on the police officer's "suspicion" alone, and then arrest and inevitably extort the young man. This is now completely legal!

As if that is not outrageous enough, subsection K effectively gives the police the power to arrest people without warrant or court order based on nothing more than a suspicion that they may be planning to commit a crime. In case the implication of this subsection is not clear enough, it bears reiteration – anyone in Nigeria can now legally be arrested for absolutely no reason whatsoever, with no basis for suspicion whatsoever, except a police officer's opinion that they may be planning to commit an offense. Nigeria now officially practises predictive policing, only without algorithms or data – just the subjective opinion on any police officer, depending on what side of the bed they wake up on.

Expansion of Arbitrary Stop and Search Powers

Section 49 takes the ludicrous expansion of police powers to the next level, empowering police officers to stop and search at random in any public place without any specified reason, parameters or conditions guiding such activity.

49.   (1) A police officer may exercise the power to stop and search in any:

      (a) place the public or any section of the public has access, on payment or otherwise, as of right or by virtue of express or implied permission; or

      (b) other place to which the public has ready access at the time when he

proposes to exercise the power but which is not a private residence.

(2) A Police officer may detain and search any person or vehicle where:

      (a) reasonable grounds for suspicion exist that the person being suspected is having in his possession; or conveying in any manner anything which he has reason to believe to have been stolen or otherwise unlawfully obtained;

      (b) reasonable grounds for suspicion exist that such person or vehicle is carrying an unlawful article;

      (c) reasonable grounds for suspicion that incidents involving serious violence may take place within a locality;

      (d) information has been received as to a description of an article being carried or of a suspected offender; and

      (e) a person is carrying a certain type of article at an unusual time or in a place where a number of burglaries or thefts are known to have taken place recently.

(3) If, in the course of a search, a police officer discovers an article which he has reasonable grounds for suspecting to be a stolen or prohibited article, he may seize it.

The nonsense of detention and search based on nothing other than a police officer's "suspicion" again rears its head in sub-section 2 where it says that police officers may stop and search any person or vehicle who they **think** may be conveying something stolen.

In other words, the regular scenario of crooked

police stopping and accusing young men who have committed no offense of being internet fraudsters, and then extorting money from them before letting them go now has legal backing. Nigerian law has effectively legalised corrupt policing and the extent to which this statement is true will be seen as the bill is explored further down the page.

Section 52, subsection 3 states that if a suspect has been arrested (an innocent young man with an iPhone for example), the police is empowered to search him "If there are reasonable grounds for believing that he has on his person any stolen items."

52. (1) Where a suspect is arrested by a police officer or a private person, the police officer making the arrest or to whom the private person hands over the suspect may search the suspect if the police officer has reasonable grounds for believing that the arrested person may present a danger to himself or others.

(2) A police officer shall also have the power in any such case to search the arrested person for anything:

(a) which he might use to assist him to escape from lawful custody; or

(b) which might be evidence relating to an offence.

(3) Where an arrested suspect is admitted to bail and bail is furnished, he shall not be searched unless there are reasonable grounds for believing that he has on his person any:

(a) stolen article;

(b) instrument of violence or poisonous substance;

(c) tools connected with the kind of offence which he is alleged to have committed; or

(d) other articles which may furnish evidence against him in regard to the offence, which he is alleged to have committed.

(4) The power to search conferred under subsection (2) is only a power to search to the extent that is reasonably required for the purpose of discovering anything or evidence.

In other words, yet again, a completely undefined and fully subjective, sweeping power has been written into law. Say for example, corrupt Nigerian police stop a young man driving his vehicle and decide to "suspect" him of internet fraud, he can then be arrested and searched to see what he has on him. Sub-subsection C then references "tools connected with the kind of offense he is alleged to have committed," so if he has an iPhone or a laptop on him, that becomes evidence of a crime and by default he is criminalised.

This is how using passive, innocent-sounding words, this bill enables all kinds of police atrocities against Nigerians, giving police officers the power to be on-the-spot judge, jury and executioner based on nothing more than their famously well-educated and informed personal viewpoints and opinions.

This is reiterated in Section 86 where yet again the police are given powers to arrest anyone, anywhere at any time without recourse to any sort of legal process based on nothing more than whatever they feel like at that moment in time.

86   Notwithstanding the provisions of this Bill or any other law relating to arrest, a police officer on a reasonable suspicion of a plan to commit an offence, may arrest, without orders from a magistrate and without warrant, the suspect where it appears to the officer that the commission of the offence cannot otherwise be prevented.

In comparison, the UK Police and Criminal Evidence Act 1984 which contains clauses about warrantless detention goes into great detail to explain and clearly define what powers are available and under what circumstances they can be used, and how to define the individuals on whom they are used.

[F1 24   Arrest without warrant: constables

(1)   A constable may arrest without a warrant—

(a)   anyone who is about to commit an offence;

(b)   anyone who is in the act of committing an offence;

(c)   anyone whom he has reasonable grounds for suspecting to be about to commit an offence;

(d)   anyone whom he has reasonable grounds for suspecting to be committing an offence.

(2)   If a constable has reasonable grounds for suspecting that an offence has been committed, he may arrest without a warrant anyone whom he has reasonable grounds to suspect of being guilty of it.

(3)   If an offence has been committed, a constable may arrest without a warrant—

(a)   anyone who is guilty of the offence;

(b)   anyone whom he has reasonable grounds for suspecting to be guilty of it.

(4)   But the power of summary arrest conferred by subsection (1), (2) or (3) is exercisable only if the constable has reasonable grounds for believing that for any of the reasons mentioned in subsection (5) it is necessary to arrest the person in question.

(5)   The reasons are—

(a)   to enable the name of the person in question to be ascertained (in the case where the constable does not know, and cannot readily ascertain, the person's name, or has reasonable grounds for doubting whether a name given by the person as his name is his real name);

(b)   correspondingly as regards the person's address;

(c)   to prevent the person in question—

(i)   causing physical injury to himself or any other person;

(ii)   suffering physical injury;

(iii)   causing loss of or damage to property;

(iv)   committing an offence against public decency (subject to subsection (6)); or

(v)   causing an unlawful obstruction of the highway;

(d)   to protect a child or other vulnerable person from the person in question;

(e)   to allow the prompt and effective investigation of the offence or of the conduct of the person in question;

(f)   to prevent any prosecution for the offence from being hindered by the disappearance of the person in question.

(6)   Subsection (5)(c)(iv) applies only where members of the public going about their normal business cannot reasonably be expected to avoid the person in question.]

Bail is NOT free after all

In Section 63, the next steps of the corrupt policing enterprise described above are then laid out in lurid detail.

52. (1) Where a suspect has been taken into police custody without a warrant for an offence other than an offence punishable with death, an officer in charge of a police station shall inquire into the case and release the suspect arrested on bail subject to subsection (2) of this section, and where it will not be practicable to bring the suspect before a court having jurisdiction with respect to the offence alleged, within 24 hours after the arrest.

(2) The police officer in charge of a police station shall release the suspect on bail on his entering into a recognisance with or without sureties for a reasonable amount of money to appear before the court or at the police station at the time and place named in the recognizance.

(3) Where a suspect is taken into custody and it appears to the police officer in charge of the station that the offence is of a capital nature, the arrested suspect shall be detained in custody, and the police officer may refer the matter to the Attorney-General of the Federation or of a State, as the case may be, for legal advice and cause the suspect to be taken before a court having jurisdiction with respect to the offence within a reasonable time.

In plain English, what this section says is that when anyone is arrested for any offence except one involving death (such as the innocent young man accused of internet fraud based on nothing more than a police officer's all seeing third eye), this person will then be bailed within 24 hours "for a reasonable sum of money."

Once again it is important to reiterate that whenever terms like "reasonable" are used in Nigerian legislation, it is almost inevitable that they become opportunities for arbitrage. In the example above, a completely innocent young man will thus find himself obligated to pay a sum of money to bail himself for an offense that existed purely in the imagination of the police. The police will then get to decide how much that sum of money is, because **the bill does not say so.**

In case it is not clear what this is, then it should be spelled out plainly – this is a framework that deliberately enables legalised theft by the Nigeria Police Force.

The extent of the legalised shakedown becomes clearer with section 98 and 99, where it states that for the vague and undefined offense of "obstructing" a police officer, Nigerians are liable to pay a fine of N500,000. For the even less believable offense of "failing to aid or assist a police officer," Nigerians are also liable to pay a fine of N100,000.

98. A person who assaults, obstructs or resists a police officer in the discharge of his duty, or aids or incites any other person to assault, obstruct or resist a police officer or other person aiding or assisting the police officer in the discharge of his duty, commits an offence and is liable on conviction to a fine of N500,000 or imprisonment for a term of six months or both.

99. Where a person is called upon to aid and assist a police officer who is, while in the discharge of his duty, assaulted or resisted or in danger of being assaulted or resisted, and the person refuses or neglects to aid and assist, the person commits an offence and is liable on conviction to a fine of N100,000 or imprisonment for a term of three months or both.

Where does the said money go when these fines are paid? Section 91 answers:

91. (1) There is established for the Nigeria Police the Police Reward Fund (in this Bill referred to as "the Reward Fund") into which shall be paid:

   (a) all money levied by order of a senior officer on members of the police for offences against discipline;

   (b) all fines levied for assaults on members of the police;

   (c) one-third of fees paid by members of the public in respect of extracts from reports made by the police;

   (d) one-third of fees paid in accordance with Standing Orders for the services of police officers who would otherwise be off duty; and

   (e) all sums ordered to be paid into the Fund under section 86 (7) of this Bill.

(2) Subject to the rules for the time being in force under section 23 of the Finance Control and Management Act, the Reward Fund shall be applied and disbursed at the direction of the Inspector-General, based on criteria laid by the Police Service Commission:

   (a) to reward members of the police for exemplary services

   (b) for payment of ex gratia compassionate gratuities to widows or children of deceased members of the force;

   (c) for making ex gratia payments towards the funeral expenses of any member of the police who dies in the service of the police; and

   (d) for such other purpose as may be determined, by the Nigerian Police Council.

This bill has thus devised a framework to legalise corrupt policing in Nigeria by criminalising everyone instead of reforming the police. To this end it has then created a "Police Reward Fund" that in all but name serves as a way of laundering the expected proceeds from what will almost certainly be corrupt policing.

Police is not your Friend

In Section 89, the bill lays out the procedure for what should happen when the police kill someone. Throughout this section, only passing mention is made of the act itself or its legality thereof. It is treated as an administrative box-ticking exercise.

(1) Where a person appears in a police station in respect of an offence or an allegation of the commission of an offence either as an accused person or a witness, or as a relation or friend of an accused person or a witness, the duty officer or such other officer as may be authorized by the officer-in-charge of the police station shall enter in the official record book:

(a) the name of the person and his national identity number, if any;

(b) the date of birth of the person;

(c) the reason for the person's visits;

(d) the name and address of the person's next-of-kin;

(e) the exact time the person comes to the station and leaves, for everyday he visits; and

(f) any ailment or medical condition which the person has.

(2) The particulars mentioned in subsection (1) of this section shall be updated each day the person remains in custody in the police station.

(3) Where, in the discharge of the police duty, a person is shot, wounded or killed, the officer commanding the operation shall record:

(a) the number of those wounded or killed, the names of the victims or their description as much as possible; and

National Assembly Page 30 of 48

(b) efforts taken to ensure hospitalisation of the wounded or proper preservation of the dead.

In fact throughout the entire bill, no mention of any specific examples of common police misbehaviour is made, and there is no reference to any proposed punishments for such behaviour. It is worded in a way that suggests that Nigerians are the enemy and the NPF is not the extremely deformed institution it is universally known to be.

Section 100 even prescribes punishments for people who give alcohol to police on duty, as though the officers themselves do not have any responsibility in the matter. No punishment or administrative action whatsoever is prescribed for police officers who drink on duty

100. (1) While on duty, a Police Officer shall not take any intoxicating liquor, psychotropic substances or stimulants, where he does, he shall be punished in accordance with the Police disciplinary procedures.

(2) A person who:

(a) knowingly harbours or entertains, or either directly or indirectly, gives any intoxicating liquor, psychotropic substance or stimulant to any Police Officer while on duty, or permits any such Police Officer to abide or remain in his house unlawfully; except in cases of extreme urgency,

(b) by threats or by offer of money, gift, spirits, liquors, psychotropic substances or stimulants induces or attempts to induce any Police Officer to commit a breach of his duty as a Police Officer or to omit any part of such duty, commits an offence and is liable on conviction to a fine of at least N50,000.00 only.

Finally section 135 prescribed punishment for "false information against police." This section says absolutely nothing about any consequences for police misconduct including false information against members of the public, which could lead to it being construed as a silencing or intimidation tactic.

135. After investigation, the head of the Unit through the Force Public Relations Officer or Public Relations Officer of a State or the Federal Capital Territory shall forward the report and its recommendations to the Inspector- General or Commissioner of Police a State or the Federal Capital Territory who shall:

    (a) send a copy of the investigation report and recommendations to the appropriate Police or oversight authority for proper disciplinary action if the investigations reveal that the offence committed is against discipline as specified in this Bill and in the Police Regulations made under this Bill; and

    (b) where it is discovered after investigations that the complainant knowingly

gave false information against the police officer or should have reasonably known that the information is false, the complainant shall be tried according to relevant laws for the time being in force.

VII

WHITE KNIGHTS AND BLACK UNICORNS: THE TALL TALES OF MAREK ZMYSLOWSKI

"It's Africa, Stupid."

That is the name of a TED Talk that has been viewed 1.7 million times on YouTube. The speaker is a charismatic Polish entrepreneur called Marek Zmyslowski who spent 4 years working in Nigeria's startup ecosystem. To the uninitiated, he is Marek Zmyslowski, former CEO of Jovago who later founded Hotel Oga and is currently a board advisor of Launch Africa, a VC company. To those in the know however, he is 'Marek Chinedu,' a successful Polish-born entrepreneur, public speaker and master of the razzle dazzle.

An engaging storyteller who is not shy about self-promotion, Marek has built up a following over the past 7 years, aided in no small part by the wild story of his 2018 arrest by Interpol, purportedly on the orders of a Nigerian-based "Godfather". This story, the exact details of which vary considerably depending on who you ask, is documented across several parts of Marek's vast storytelling franchise. There is a Medium post that has been read tens of thousands of times. There is another viral Medium post that talks about it. He gave a TED Talk about it. He even wrote a book about it.

The basic thrust of the story according to Marek goes thus:

The protagonist and hero, a charming, good-looking Polish entrepreneur with global ambitions moves to Africa to co-found the "Amazon of Africa". After successfully launching Jumia Travel, he then moves on to found Hotel Oga, a startup with growth potential and great prospects. A certain heavyweight Nigerian-Indian investor whom we come to know as the "Godfather" comes into the picture, and the entrepreneur is convinced to accept this investment because said Godfather apparently holds the keys to regulatory favour and ease of business in Nigeria.

Like all good stories, there is a twist – a personal and professional conflict develops between the hero and the Godfather over their different visions for the company. The Godfather then does what Godfathers do, and tries to metaphorically whack him via his puppet CFO and an orchestrated boardroom hit. The hero survives because his co-founders come to his rescue, but this marks the start of an ugly conflict as the Godfather adopts tactics that belong in Mario Puzo's book. The company suffers as a result and nearly goes bankrupt.

Eventually our hero gets tired of fighting an uphill battle against this super-connected Nigerian-Indian investment whale and negotiates a sale to a major East African competitor which offers him an exit from the Godfather's African stomping ground. Unfortunately he has underestimated the sheer power and maliciousness of said Godfather, and on January 14, 2018, he is arrested at Warsaw Okecie Airport where he is told that he is the subject of an Interpol Red Notice and he is wanted in Nigeria. Apparently the Godfather's tentacles extend as far as Interpol, and he is told that he might be extradited to Nigeria.

Our hero struggles to understand how an institution like Interpol could have been compromised by a Nigerian-Indian Godfather until he realises that it accepts donations from private organisations. The obvious inference is left hanging in the air, but – possibly for legal reasons – unspoken. Upon getting out of detention, he receives 3 phone calls: the first from his Nigerian banker informing him of a police order to freeze his accounts; the second from a Nigeiran journalist with an interestingly-timed tipoff about his arrest; and the third from a lawyer representing Il Capo Tutti Nigeriano himself.

"Pay $300,000 into this unknown, nondescript account, and my boss will make all your problems go away," says the female voice on the phone.

Despite learning from two other startup founders in Nigeria that his experience in the Godfather's hands is not unique, and despite the entire Nigerian legal and law enforcement apparatus being at the beck and call of said all-powerful man, our hero decides to fight his case in court – a Nigerian court no less. The fresh-faced, idealistic European kid thus goes up against the battle-hardened, cash-loaded, worldly wise Godfather in his own backyard – and he somehow pulls off a stunning victory! On July 23, 2018, the court rules in his favour and just like in any good story, there is emotional closure as the good guy wins and faith is restored in humanity.

As unlikely as it is gripping, it is a story that thousands of people around the world have read, watched and listened to Marek Zmyslowski tell over and over. From time to time, its contents are vigorously disputed by people with knowledge of the matter, but it has always been difficult to establish any coherent counter-story. This is mainly because the "Godfather" and his conniving CFO puppet have not come out swinging like Marek. In the court of public opinion, it is often the person who gets the most words in that wins by default. Right from February 2019 when Marek began telling this story, this has always been the case.

Until now.

The Godfather and his Friends – Not Quite As Portrayed

When you think of the "Godfather" in Marek's story, you would probably imagine someone who looks like the conceptual offspring of Amitabh Bachchan and Aliko Dangote – a stern faced industrialist and seasoned political operator whose eyes have watched many a horse head being placed at the foot of a rival's bed over the decades.

Horse beheading aside, Maneesh Garg would appear to satisfy all these parameters. He is the seasoned industrialist you have probably never heard of, who has over 27 years of experience in various Nigerian sectors including chemicals, commodities, healthcare, supply chain management and integrated logistics. Since quitting a job with the World Bank in 1993 to join his family business in Nigeria, he has transformed Nagode Industries into Afriglobal Group, a multi-sector behemoth with an annual turnover in excess of N30 billion. There are possibly some things that he does not know about operating a business in Nigeria, but in all probability, they are not very many.

That however, is where all the similarities between the Godfather of Marek's story and the real life Nigerian-Indian investor end. In reality as I discovered while digging into him, Maneesh Garg's main skill as a businessman appears to be knowing what sectors to target, followed by silent, ruthless execution and a keen eye for further investment opportunities – as against whacking people. Also as he revealed in the TED Talk below, he has found himself inside a cell at Kirikiri Prison over a business debt – hardly the calling card of a super-connected Nigerian "godfather."

You could describe him as an experienced

entrepreneur or even a powerful investor. "Godfather" would appear to be pushing it a bit.

The CFO, for whom special words of contempt are reserved in Marek's story, is Gulbet Kiros, an American citizen of Eritrean and Ethiopian descent. Kiros, who has lived and worked in Nigeria since 2014, is the Co-Founder and CEO of Faya Media Inc, a cloud-based advertising management platform for media buying and selling. Completing the list of the Godfather's henchmen in the story is Edmund Olotu, founder of Techadvance, a startup offering Business Process Outsourcing, payment and data management solutions. Kiros and Olotu are also co-founders of Ferox Partners, a company that plays an important role in this story.

Olotu had previously responded to Marek's story with a Medium post of his own, which was later taken down. Marek claims that Olotu removed the post because it contained libelous claims. Olotu insists that he did no such thing, and that it was in fact Marek who got Medium to remove the post by making a copyright claim on an image of his book cover which was included in the post.

The full and unredacted cache of materials I got my hands on while researching this story are far too voluminous to fit on this page. They include bank statements, board meeting minutes, payment receipts, invoices, e-mail exchanges, corporate registration documents and legal notices. As a compromise I have included only relevant screenshots in this article. Every screenshot will be linked to a PDF version of the full document where it was taken from.

When placed side-by-side with Marek's claims, the documents often tell a different story altogether to the one that has gone around the world twice, but ultimately my opinion is immaterial. Marek has told his story. Now for the first time, we get to see the metaphorical receipts in great detail, as well as hear from Gulbet Kiros, the CFO and alleged henchman of "The Godfather" directly. Then it is up to the reader to draw any conclusions.

The Shareholder Agreement and the Polish Company

The fundamental origin of the conflict between Marek and his adversaries lies in the contents of a Shareholder Agreement (SHA) that brought Maneesh into Hotel Oga as a board member and shareholder. Under the terms of this SHA which can be viewed here, Maneesh uses his investment vehicle, Marathon Real Estate. Marek claims that this SHA is completely invalid and that he has never acknowledged or recognised it. He also claims that his agreement was with Maneesh personally. As such, he contends that the listing of Marathon Real Estate in the SHA is proof that it is invalid.

IN WITNESS WHEREOF this Shareholders' Agreement has been executed in the manner hereinafter appearing the day and year first above written.

Executed as a deed by MARATHON REAL ESTATE LIMITED acting by MANEESH GARG, a director, in the presence of: .... SIGNATURE OF WITNESS PATIEN OF ELISE LAWYER NAME, ADDRESS AND OCCUPATION OF WITNESS	*Maneesh Garg*
Executed as a deed by HOSPITALITY TECHNOLOGY SOLUTIONS LIMITED acting by MAREK ZMYSLOWSKI, a director, in the presence of: .... SIGNATURE OF WITNESS NAME, ADDRESS AND OCCUPATION OF WITNESS	
Executed as a deed by MAREK ZMYSLOWSKI in the presence of: .... SIGNATURE OF WITNESS NAME, ADDRESS AND OCCUPATION OF WITNESS	

26

Marek's signature on the disputed SHA

The validity of this SHA forms the basis for most of the argument put forward by the creditors turned investors. Based on this agreement they say, they documented their ownership share in Hotel Oga and all its intellectual property (IP) at home and abroad. Kiros insists that no other SHA exists and alleges that Marek is simply lying through his teeth. As can be seen above, this SHA appears to have Marek's signature on it. Furthermore this May 2016 email exchange between Marek and Kiros clearly shows Marek agreeing to terms of investment from Ferox Partners.

**(May 27, 2016) Kiros' Original Investment Terms

From: Marek Zmyslowski <marek@hotel.oga.com>
Date: Fri, May 27, 2016 at 5:27 AM
Subject: Re: kilka danych do porownania
To: KirosG

agreed

Pozdrawiam / Best regards / Mit freundlichen Grußen

Marek Zmyslowski
Founder & CEO HotelOga

LinkedIn | Twitter | Skype: marek.zmyslowski

On May 26, 2016, at 23:49, Kiros Gulbet wrote:

Marek

Below is the updated terms we agreed to during our last dinner at Spice in Lagos. Please let me know if you have any comments or changes you want to make

- 5% that vests over six months = Consideration for this will be 10K plus Advisory work. [We need to agree from which month this becomes in effect. You had mentioned starting the date from around the date we want to addix or we could do April or you can suggest from the date you deem fair]

- An additional 10%, if I get us funded at 10m valuation within the next 12 months. This excludes the bridge financing and it assumes you will execute on the strategies to get us there. We will agree to this strategy and start marketing it to investors by end of Q3. Lastly, this 10% is just an economic stake and non-voting to accommodate your concern about control.

Best,

Kiros

Here are the publicly verifiable facts:

As confirmed by Marek, he was the CEO of both Hotel Online, a hotel indexing and booking online startup registered in Poland, and Hotel Oga, an identical company registered in Nigeria. Both companies used intellectual property and operating infrastructure owned by Hotel Online. Under the terms of the settlement agreement however, Maneesh and Kiros were recognised as investors and shareholders in both entities, and thus part owners who were entitled to a percentage of their total share value.

Marek however, claims that both entities were separate and the Hotel Oga investors had no claim on the assets of Hotel Online. In what will become a recurring feature in this story, the investors categorically insist that this is a flat out lie. I was able to get my hands on an email exchange and the minutes of a board meeting from 2016 that appear to show Marek not only acknowledging that the Nigerian shareholders expected value from both entities, but also agreeing to collapse both Nigerian and Polish business entities into one as instructed by the board.

02/2016

Minutes of Meeting of the Directors of Hospitality Technology Solutions Ltd. Held at Eleganza Plaza, Suite 2, 33, Mobolaji Johnson Avenue Oregun Industrial Layout Ikeja, Lagos on Wednesday 17th August, 2016 at 3.00pm

Present

| Mr. Maneesh Garg | - Chairman |
| Mr. Marek Zmyslowski | - Director / CEO |

In Attendance

Mr. Toyin Fatunmbi   - Toyin Fatunmbi & Co. (Chartered Accountants) – Took the minutes

Absent

Mrs. Omolara Adagunodo   - Director

The Board after deliberation resolved as follows:

S/N	Issue	Action	Who	When
1.0	Matters arising from minutes of meeting of 20th April 2016	Proprietary rights to HotelOga Software		
		a) The CEO is to incorporate the Mauritius entity and the Poland entity of Hospitality Technology Solutions Ltd; and	Marek	30/09/2016
		b) Get agreement signed between the Mauritius entity and the Poland entity to make the HotelOga software developed by the Poland entity the property of Hospitality Technology Solutions Ltd, Mauritius	Marek	30/09/2016
		Ownership transfer / documentation should be done for Company's assets purchased in CEO's name.	Marek	30/09/2016
		Implementation of Personal Income Tax and Post-employment benefits for employees on hold till the company gets the next round of funding.	Marek	10/11/2016
2.0	Review of Financial Statements for the period ended 31 July, 2016	a) Additional revenue numbers for June and July from OTAs that were not linked to HotelOga App to be incorporated in the financial statement.	Toyin	10/09/2016
		b) Prepare estimate of performance targets for August to December 2016 covering the following areas.	Marek	21/08/2016

The real smoking gun however, is when I get access to a cache of Hotel Oga's internal files including a document showing Hotel Oga paying salaries for Hotel Online staff in Poland. At this point, Marek's story of greedy African investors trying to steal the IP of a plucky Polish entrepreneur starts to look increasingly tenuous. Why would a separate Nigerian company that has no connection with the Polish company have the Polish company's staff salaries on its books?

The only explanation that could possibly explain these disparities is that these documents are not genuine. If they are, then major holes have already started to appear in the Black Unicorn saga.

Marek's other claim that purportedly invalidates those of Ferox and Marathon is that he registered Hotel

Oga in February 2016. He has previously posted this document online as proof of this claim.

We, the several persons whose names, addresses are subscribed, are desirous of being formed into a company in pursuance of this Memorandum of Association and we respectively agree to take the number of shares in the Capital of the company set opposite our respective names.

S/N	Names, Addresses & Description of Subscribers	No. of Shares Taken by Each Subscriber	Signature
1	MAREK ZMYSLOWSKI 15, WOLE OLATEJU CRESCENT LEKKI LAGOS, LAGOS STATE. (DIRECTOR)	7,900,000	SIGNED
2	(DIRECTOR)	2,000,000	SIGNED
3	(DIRECTOR)	100,000	SIGNED

DATED this ____ Day of ____ 2016

Witness to the above Signatures:

Name: EZEOGU JENNIFER

Address: NO. 4, TAMARASSET CLOSE, OFF AGADEZ CRESCENT, WUSE II, ABUJA

Occupation: LEGAL PRACTITIONER

The documents I saw however, suggest something entirely different. Below is a CAC registration document from 2015 for Hospitality Technology Solutions (Hotel Oga's trading name). This document it turns out, also has Marek's signature on it. Once again, it is either the document is not genuine or Marek has significantly misstated the true state of affairs.

I sighted a Polish registration document for Hotel Online which shows that it was registered in 2015. Given that Marek claims to have registered both companies in

2016, both stories can definitely not be true at the same time. Also tellingly, there is a document showing that investment inflows from Maneesh into HTS started in 2015.

INVESTMENT OF NAGODE INDUSTRIES LIMITED IN HOSPITALITY SOLUTIONS TECHNOLOGY LTD
AS AT 31 JULY 2016

Create Date	Effective Date	Description/ Payee/Memo	Amount (Currency)	Ex. Rate	Amount (NGN)
9/9/2015	8/9/2015	201509080006636//201509080006636// FX RECV'D OB CHEVAL COMMODITIERS DMCC	USD	200.00	NGN
2/2/2016	2/2/2016	TRF FRM NAGODE INDUSTRIES LIMITED	NGN	1.00	NGN
3/3/2016	3/3/2016	ZB CQ 3007/NAGODE IND LTD	NGN	1.00	NGN
12/4/2016	12/4/2016	INFLOW FROM NAGODE INDUSTRIES LTD	NGN	1.00	NGN
		Total			NGN

When I spoke to Kiros, he claimed that what really drove a wedge between Marek and Maneesh was Marek's routing of company finances through Poland. The following documents show an odd arrangement where booking revenue from Expedia would not be paid into Hotel Oga's account in Nigeria, but would be paid in Hotel Online's account in Poland. From there it would be remitted through Marek's personal account to Nigeria where it would then be logged as a loan on the company's books.

From: Marek Zmyslowski [mailto:marek@hoteloga.com]
Sent: 24 August 2016 10:47 AM
To: Maneesh Garg
Cc: Toyin Fatunmbi
Subject: Re: HotelOga

Maneesh,

The revenue is not captured in Poland yet - It was the concept I sent him after my discussion with tax advisors.
When I met him, we were still not quite sure yet how to do it the optimal way, and we're still tweaking the plan.
It involves US (Expedia is US based) and EU and Nigeria so it's quite complex.
Everything we are working on is part of seetting up the main entity in Mauritius. We should be certain how its
should work in the following months and I can present you it on next board meeting.

I think we shouldn't pursue ████ anymore. His answer shows he doesn't really get the concept of investing
early stage in tech startups. I don't want sb like that as my investor.

Pozdrawiam / Best regards / Mit freundlichen Grüßen

Marek Zmyslowski
Founder & CEO HotelOga
www.hoteloga.com

Linkedin | Twitter | Skype: marek.zmyslowski

Proper Date	Week	Description/ Payee/Memo	CREDIT	DEBIT	Categories
06-05-2016	19	loan	500,000.00		
08-05-2016	20	loan	1,000,000.00		
08-05-2016	20	loan	150,000.00		
10-06-2016	24	loan	500,000.00		
10-06-2016	24	second loan	501,000.00		
10-06-2016	24	loan3	502,000.00		
10-06-2016	24	loan4	504,000.00		
21-06-2016	26	loan	1,500,000.00		
04-07-2016	28	loan July	2,000,000.00		
04-07-2016	28	salary margaret minus loan//NEFT TRF TO O		100,000.00	Personnel
13-07-2016	29	loan	510,000.00		
21-07-2016	30	loan	500,000.00		
28-07-2016	31	loan	2,000,000.00		
01-08-2016	32	ISW CHARGE: ISW2540460-salary plus loan august//DLU/W		100.00	Payment cost
01-08-2016	32	ISW2540460-salary plus loan august//OL		270,000.00	Personnel
01-08-2016	32	salary august minus loan//NEFT TRF TO OY		100,000.00	Personnel
08-08-2016	33	loan	500,000.00		
08-08-2016	33	loan	300,000.00		
28-08-2016	36	loan	3,000,000.00		
05-09-2016	37	loan	1,300,000.00		
06-09-2016	37	salary k minus loan//NEFT TRF TO O		70,000.00	Personnel
09-09-2016	37	loan	1,000,000.00		
11-09-2016	38	loan	1,000,000.00		
21-10-2016	43	loan	400,000.00		
26-10-2016	44	loan	3,000,000.00		
27-10-2016	44	loan	300,000.00		
			20,967,000.00	540,100.00	

Marek has previously shared screenshots of transactions that appear to show him transferring naira amounts cumulatively worth $165,000 to Hotel Oga. These documents appear to indicate that these funds were in fact never actually his, but were merely set up to pass through his account. And all of this is really just for starters as the story embarks on a winding journey down a rabbit hole of questionable financial management, poor corporate governance and ultimately the involvement of law enforcement.

Expensive Habits and Missing Money

When looking at the background material for the story, it is clear that Marek projects the air of a self-confident investor and a net contributor to Nigeria's tech space and economy. He went as far as sharing the invoice online, as proof that he paid his own rental expenses and was not in fact an expensive burden to company finances as Olotu had claimed.

The problem with this is that one of the documents in the cache I accessed strongly suggests that something else entirely took place. The bank statement below from 2016 clearly shows Hotel Oga paying for Marek's flat as well as making several unexplained cash payments to his personal account.

I reached out to the company's erstwhile auditor, Toyin Fatunmbi to confirm the veracity of the documents in this story. He informed me that while for professional reasons he could not comment about the documents directly, he did however completely trust my source whom I named to him. I put the question to Kiros and his theory is that Marek must have requested an invoice from the company, ostensibly for his personal records, only to later put it out on the internet as proof of his non-freeloading ways.

It must be noted at this point that I have never actually met Marek Zmyslowski in person. Apart from a few whispered rumours from some of his former employees about his allegedly less-than-professional behaviour and my personal observation of his obvious desire to brand himself as a rock star founder, I had never until recently had any cause to disbelieve anything he said or wrote about his time in Nigeria.

When I started looking through the incredibly detailed web of payment receipts, bank records, registration documents and email exchanges, this started to change significantly. The document below for example, tells a very familiar story about poor corporate governance, typified by the "Business Meeting and Entertainment" expenses over a 4-month period in 2016.

While Marek insists that he put his own funds into Hotel Oga and it was "the Godfather" whose greed and ambition forced him to exit, Kiros insists that he was in fact living parasitically off the company, all the while also commanding a relatively high salary, with his rent, car and living expenses paid for by the company.

The email exchange below typifies the level of support that Marek enjoyed from his investors at Hotel Oga. Stating that he did not have a U.S. account to receive funds in, Marek convinced one of them to send him a $10,000 personal loan through his fiancée's U.S. account

With every new internal Hotel Oga document I looked though, a new picture emerged of Marek Zmyslowski. As against the clean-cut Polish heartthrob who fell in love with Nigeria to the point of adopting the name "Chinedu" only to become the victim of a ruthless gang-up, it starts to look like he may in fact be the one who led a gang-up of his own. The documents portray someone who could well be a perfectly capable entrepreneur when he feels like it, but who carries out a litany of questionable actions that raise several red flags.

My lengthy oral and written correspondence with Kiros yielded several anecdotes about his time working with Marek – many of them too colourful to go on record – but this quote from a written statement he sent to me stands out as a summary of his experience:

> **"Marek is a great sales guy and a silver-tongued storyteller. He has a great instinct for promotion and marketing. However, his weakness was apparent when it came to management, strategy, and execution. The latter requires attention to detail, discipline, and focus. Unfortunately, those shortcomings and his lack of self-awareness and an ingrained sense of entitlement would become his undoing. Worse, when**

you overpromise and under-deliver consistently, you lose credibility and expose your incompetence and/or inexperience. Especially when you are vain and insecure, you start doing irrational, and if not criminal, things, to preserve the illusion."

< **Tweet**

Marek Zmyslowski ✔
@marekchinedu

There's only one downside of being a white tall handsome guy...oh sorry, there's actually none.

03/12/2017, 2:21 PM from Ukraine

2 Retweets **15** Likes

It was this tendency toward the unethical he says, that brought Marek into open confrontation with him after he came in as Hotel Oga's full time CFO early October 2016 in an attempt to stem leakages and institute proper financial controls like daily reporting of revenue directly to board level. One of the things he claims he discovered was evidence of under-remittance under the odd arrangement of sending revenue from Nigeria via Poland back to Nigeria via Marek's personal account.

I took a look at the November 2016 Cash Management Report and I spotted a few things that would appear to corroborate Kiros's claim. For example, if you look at the report and focus on October alone, you will see that Marek remitted or "lent" N3.7 million. The problem is that according to Hotel Online Bank Statements, the money sent that month was $13,000, which means that at the official rate of N315-$1, this figure should have been N4.09 million. At the then black market rate of N363-$1, the figure should have been N4.72 million. This means anything from N300,000 to N1,000,000 disappeared into a financial black hole somewhere between Marek's account and the company's account just for the month of October alone.

Marek has not offered any explanation for the discrepancy or even referenced his unusual cash warehousing arrangement with Hotel Oga.

Eventually, when tensions between both men came to a head, Marek tried to politely fire the CFO by suggesting that he should resign and focus on his duties as a board member. According to Kiros, he would have done exactly that, were it not for the fact that the safety of his own investment was tied to Maneesh, who in turn wanted him there to keep an eye on Marek.

M Gmail

HotelOga - Kiros moving forward
1 message

Marek Zmyslowski <marek@hoteloga.com>   Thu, Dec 29, 2016 at 2:08 AM
To: Gulbet Kiros <kiros@hoteloga.com>,

Hey Man

Let me start by stating that HotelOga is now is in a very challenging situation with the Dubai guys opting out, most
probably after they were not pushed enough by Maneesh,
which suggests he's also not super helpful, which means he's not happy with HotelOga. Which is another issue.

Additional, counterproductive, potential complication with you is the last thing HotelOga (and me) needs right now.
So I'm aiming here to find the best and the simplest solution, satisfying both you and me.

We both have totally different backgrounds and look differently at building startups. This should result in great synergy but
somehow the effects are something totally opposite.
Me acting as asshole is one thing. Us not being able to find common ground and work flow is another one, I guess I also
failed in managing our expectations towards each other (probably with Maneesh as well.
It would be also probably easier if we worked in the same office, and if you were 100% focused on HotelOga.
Unfortunately we don't have that luxury now.
All are good lessons for the future.

Regarding the action pivot plan for the next 3months for HotelOga:
1 I will probably cut the staff by 3-4 ppl in Nigeria
2 We focus on big hotels only and probably let go the costly not performing hotels
3 We immediately start acquisition in Ghana and EA (only PRIO hotels) - we do it without opening offices there, we use
infrastructure and sales force of our Indian investor in EA
4 We are dropping the payment handling cases for prepayment bookings (like Expedia) because we have no working
capital for this
5 We are immediately introducing POSes for Hotels (like Simtrader) because that will actually allow us to collect our
commisions much faster.
6 We are finishing setting up new entity - I'm taking lead on this. After many talks and giving it a fault, I want to do it in
Delaware in the end. Have many reasons for this - however still happy to talk if you think it's a bad idea. I will take care of
the legal stuff for it, as well as managing the transition and keeping our investors happy about the process.

Re: Your Role in the company moving forward.
From CFO and Investor I suggest transition to Investor and Advisor. We would need to come up with a nice story about
the reason of such.
I'm OK with you having access to all necessary information about how the company is doing, just like every other
investor.
I value your input, I just don't see us working on a daily basis. I will have to hire ASAP a more senior CFO, based in
Nigeria or Poland. He will take your responsibility of dealing with Fatunimbi.
As for investors, I'd like to ask you help me still manage Maneesh and his expertetions.
For the rest of contacts and ongoing discussion, I will take lead on them.

Marek Goes Rogue

At this point in the timeline of Hotel Oga's eventual
demise, there was an email exchange between Gulbet
Kiros and Maciej Prostak, Marek's Polish cofounder. As
can be seen in the attached conversation transcript this
conversation did not go well at all. In January 2017, the
relationship between Marek and Kiros deteriorated even
further, principally because of what Kiros alleges, was
Marek's unilateral decision to borrow N22 million from
a newly-launched micro credit startup called Lidya – and
this is where the story gets really interesting.

According to this spreadsheet, Lidya was charging Hotel Oga annualised interest rates going from 55 percent to as much as 206 percent. Even worse, I then spotted an email exchange between Marek and Kiros on January 24, 2017 where Marek asked his CFO and board member to make a payment to Lidya without an invoice. This apparently was where Kiros had finally had enough and finally drew the line.

---------- Forwarded message ----------
From: **Gulbet Kiros** <kiros@hoteloga.com>
Date: Tue, Jan 24, 2017 at 6:23 PM
Subject: Fwd: Lidya Loan Repayment Details
To: Gulbet Kiros

FYI

---------- Forwarded message ----------
From: **Itunu Efunkoya** <itunu.efunkoya@lidya.co>
Date: Tue, Jan 24, 2017 at 12:23 PM
Subject: Re: Lidya Loan Repayment Details
To: Marek Zmyslowski <marek@hoteloga.com>, kiros@hoteloga.com
Cc: Oye Fajobi <oye.fajobi@lidya.co>, Ercin Eksin <ercin.eksin@lidya.co>, Tunde Kehinde <tunde.kehinde@lidya.co>

Hi Kiros,

Please find attached an official document detailing the loan payments due today.

Regards,

On Tue, Jan 24, 2017 at 8:45 AM, Marek Zmyslowski <marek@hoteloga.com> wrote:
Hey Kiros,
There is no invoice for this, I'll explain you later in the day when we see in the office how this works, for now just pls make the payment to the account given by lidya

Sent from mobile device

On 23 Jan 2017, at 17:25 Itunu Efunkoya <itunu.efunkoya@lidya.co> wrote:
Hello Marek,

Please find below the new repayment amount for tomorrow with the service charge adjusted accordingly.

In his written account, Kiros says:

"I said no to paying without an invoice. I would also add that the investors couldn't understand how he borrowed so much at absurd rates with board approval (per SHA rules) nor could they understand how Lydia extended credit without any documentation, not to mention take a 22MM risk on a start-up. Furthermore, his refusal to terminate the relationship, even when the investors offered the same credit terms, raised suspension and tensions about the arrangement. This seems to be justified given that Lidya co-founder, Ercin, personally transferred 5K USD as seed money, right after Kiros paid the first invoice submitted by Lydia."

Marek's response was as swift as it was sudden. On February 3, 2017, he unceremoniously fired Kiros as Hotel Oga CFO – a decision that predictably did not go down well at board level. A CEO firing a board member from a position within the company is an exceptional occurrence to say the least.

Marek Zmyslowski ✔ @marekchin... · 15h ⌄
Congrats to Lidya! (Altough whoever had an issue with Jumia being called African, should have an issue with Lidya being called Nigerian) Nigerian Fintech Firm Targets $1.1 Billion in Eastern Europe Loans

Nigerian Fintech Firm Targets $1.1 Billion in Eastern Europe Loans
bloomberg.com

Kiros believes that the odd financing agreement between Hotel Oga and Lidya was the result of a back-channel agreement between Marek and Ercin to indirectly seed Lidya and gather traction for its funding round.

The timeline below showing the period between the Lidya loan facility and Lidya's successful funding round fits well with Kiros's theory.

Lidya's Key Growth Milestones

More importantly, shortly after Kiros's ouster, Marek then secretly concluded plans to sell Hotel Oga to Savannah Sunrise, a Kenyan competitor. Neither Kiros nor Maneesh were informed about this and in fact it was whistleblowers within the company who reached out to the board with written evidence of the deal from Marek's Slack conversation with Maciej.

THE JUNGLE

LETTER OF INTENT

by and between:

Hotel Online Sp. z o.o. with its registered seat in Warsaw, at ul. Szpitalna 1/11, 00 – 020 Warsaw, entered in the National Register of Entrepreneurs maintained by the District Court for the capital city of Warsaw in Warsaw, 12th Commercial Division of the National Court Register (KRS) under number KRS 0000583178, Tax Identification Number NIP: 5252635060, National Business Registry Number REGON: 382937025, hereinafter referred to as **"HotelOga"** represented, in compliance with the rules of representation disclosed in the National Register of Entrepreneurs, b/ ███████████████ – **President of the Management Board,**

and

Savanna Sunrise the company incorporated under the laws of Ras Al Khaimah, UAE, with its registered seat in Dubai, UAE at: Office 1100B, Al Habtoor Motors Building, Sheikh Zayed Road, registered with RAK Investment Authority under number 10/14/9426, hereinafter referred to as **"Savanna Sunrise"**

HotelOga and **Savanna Sunrise** shall hereinafter jointly be referred to as "Parties".

Considering that:

A. HotelOga and Savanna Sunrise conduct similar commercial activities

B. The Parties are interested in the merger of the two companies by means of Savanna Sunrise acquiring all the shares in HotelOga, compensating the current shareholders through the issue of new shares. The merged company shall hereinafter be referred to as "the Company".

C. Summing up initial findings regarding the merger of the companies carried out by the Parties, the Parties decided to sign the Letter of Intent (the "LOI")

1. The Parties mutually undertake to conduct negotiations as outlined in this LOI in good faith and taking into account interests of the other Party and in compliance with good practices.

2. ███
██
███████████████████████████████████████ The new shares shall be

5. The Parties shall participate in the share capital of the Company in the same ratio and under the same conditions, ie., each Party will take 50% (fifty percent) of the share capital of the Company and the subscription of shares will take place at the same valuation for each of the Parties

6. All offices, branches and organizational units of the Parties, with its seat in the countries where the Parties conduct commercial activity shall become organizational units of the newly created entity at the time of the merger and will operate under its company name.

7.

8. The Parties agree that further decisions on the merger will have to obtain the unanimous consent of the main founders of the Parties. It means that each agreement will require a joint consent given by:

   8.1. Marek Zmyslowski

   8.2. Maciej Prostak

   8.3. Endre Opdal

   8.4. Håvar Bauck.

9.

10. At the same time the Parties undertake to rapidly conclude on whether there is sufficient common ground to assume that the Transaction shall reach completion. In the event of a positive conclusion, the parties shall, from that time forth, agree to jointly seek investors interested in the acquisition of shares of the Company, in the frame of the planned issue of shares of series A.

11. The Parties undertake to consider as confidential any information not already publicly available in the framework of the negotiation procedure. Any confidential information held by either party may only be used in connection with the merger process stipulated in this LOI, and may not be shared with any external party, except financial institutions and/or advisers specifically involved in the process. Even in the aforementioned cases, the sharing of information shall be subject to agreement between the Parties, and to the signing of a non-disclosure agreement by the external party. At the same time the Parties stipulate that the obligation of confidentiality applies to each of the Parties for a period of negotiation and the period of three (3) years after the end of

After finding out that Marek was planning to sell the company behind his investors' backs, this email exchange involving Marek, Maneesh, Edmund and Kiros then ensued. The outcome as acknowledged by Marek below was a new shareholding structure which gave Maneesh a further $40,000 worth of Hotel Oga shares in exchange for buying out $40,000 of Kiros's shares. Documents informing Savannah about the settlement were also dispatched. This was done with the understanding that the Savannah deal would still go ahead, in which case Maneesh's investment in Hotel Oga would be fully documented and he would get full payment from Savannah for his investment.

Marek Zmyslowski <marek@hoteloga.com>   Mon, Feb 20 2017 at 12:17 PM
To: Gulbet Kiros
Cc: Maneesh Garg   , Omuli Iwere   "Michael Onmobi

sorry, updating one number (Was wrong about maneesh number):

Dear Kiros.
Thanks for the call and I'm glad we are getting somewhere.

Dear Omuli, pls prepare paperwork according to our offer:

1. Maneesh terminates loan agreement with Kiros, in return gets shares with the value of **40k USD** in both polish and nigerian HotelOga entity.
[Quoted text hidden]

Unknown to them, while still finalising this settlement agreement, Marek had begun secretly negotiating a sale with a South African company called Nightsbridge. As seen in the email below, on April 28, 2017, Kiros received information from a third party stating that the Savannah deal was off, Marek had sold the company to Nightsbridge, and he had not returned to Nigeria from Poland after travelling for the Easter holiday.

In his statement, Kiros describes what happened:

"While Marek & Co. were rushing to sell Hotel Oga, they were also purposely delaying signing the settlement agreement, effectively robbing us of our investment. If it were not for the notice I received with proof of the invoice from concerned staff on April 28, 2017, he would have stripped the company of all the assets and left us at the mercy of the courts in Poland, since by then he had sold all the company assets and traveled to Poland. This is when the lawyers rushed to file an injunction on all the accounts and sought to serve Marek the court order and petition. Despite his tale of not running away, he wasn't found at the apartment, which the company had paid for him, he didn't answer any of our calls either. Around this time, we found out that he had sold the company car and other assets, which led us to believe he fled the country. Owing to the actions highlighted above, we had to file a police petition to hold Marek accountable for such a blatant attempt to defraud his creditors and investors. Since he was not in Nigeria, the recourse available to us was to notify Interpol about the case we had filed. The Interpol petition (here) was filed in August of 2016."

JOOTS
ATTORNEYS

31 July, 2017

Deputy Inspector General of Police
Force Criminal Intelligence and Investigation Dept.
The Nigeria Police,
Area 10, Garki
Abuja-FCT

Attention: DCP INTERPOL Annex Lagos

Dear Sir,

RE: PETITION ON THEFT AND EMBEZZLEMENT OF COMPANY FUND AGAINST MR. MAREK ZMYSLOWSKI

We are Solicitors to Marathon Real Estate Limited (represented by Mr. Maneesh Garg) and Ferox Associate and Partners Limited (represented by Mr. Gulbet Kiros) *("our Clients")* who are shareholder and investor respectively in Hospitality Technology Solutions Limited (a Nigerian Information Technology Company trading under the name and style of Hotel Oga) and on their express instructions write to lay a criminal complaint on the well-orchestrated theft perpetuated by Mr. Marek Zmyslowski (hereinafter referred to as Marek).

BACKGROUND

Sometime in 2016 and early 2017, our clients were offered the opportunities to invest approximately $220,000.00 (Two Hundred and Twenty Thousand Dollars) in Hotel Oga. A Shareholders Agreement was executed between one of our client (Marathon Real Estate Limited), Marek and Hotel Oga which confirming the Investment of Marathon Real Estate Limited in Hotel Oga-**See exhibit A**. Unknown to our clients, Marek who is the Chief Executive Officer of Hotel Oga, diverted the revenues derived from the customers of Hotel Oga to a Polish entity called Hotel Online Limited without authorization from the management of Hotel Oga.

Sometime in the month of February 2017, our clients noticed that jobs executed for clients (especially those executed for Expedia (also known as Travelscape LLC- emails showing that Expedia was a client of Hotel Oga attached **as exhibit B**) were being paid to Hotel Online Limited in Poland (which also had Marek as the CEO), and these

While Marek says that he "won his case in Nigeria," no such thing in fact ever happened. His case remains open and unresolved. The case he refers to is a separate procedural case challenging the process that was used by the police to freeze his Nigerian bank accounts. While he did indeed win that case against the Nigeria Police Force, his case with Marathon Real Estate and Ferox Associates & Partners in fact remains very much open – a fact he has never publicly disclosed.

Worse still, as the email exchange below shows, many months after the Interpol notice was issued, Marek continued communicating with both investors, promising an amicable resolution of the issue, and that Maneesh would get full value for his share in Hotel Oga and Hotel Online. He even expressly acknowledged Maneesh's shareholding in both entities in this exchange.

After 4 months of negotiating a $293,000 settlement which included the value of the investment made into Hotel Oga and Hotel Online, loans given to him, legal fees and interest, Marek changed his tune. On February 19, 2018, the same day he published this viral Medium post which kick started his publicity campaign, Marek sent an email to Maneesh stating that he would no longer negotiate a settlement and his lawyer would handle matters going forward. The said lawyer then proceeded to inform Maneesh on February 22 that Marek owed no debt and the investors should sign a document waiving their claim.

Even more incredibly, while this was playing out, Marek then sent a proxy party to intercede on his behalf in Nigeria, begging Maneesh to drop the case and let Marek off the hook for the sake of Nigerian-Polish relations. The message below from the emissary even included a confidentiality agreement which the investors were apparently supposed to sign and thus gag themselves while Marek was going to town globally with his story of Nigerian 'godfathers' versus a plucky Polish upstart.

"The fact that after he publicly demonized and defamed us, he had the galls to send us a confidentiality agreement was stunning. Unfortunately, for him, I declined to participate in the fourth round of settlement talks and severed the PoA given to Maneesh to purse my own recourse and justice."

Gulbet Kiros

The Great Showman

Marek Zmyslowski has achieved great individual success by leveraging the brand he has built, which largely stems from his thrilling story of frontier capitalism in the Wild Western corner of the Dark Continent. His story has got him a book deal and several speaking engagements, plus the perceived credibility that has netted him several lucrative board and advisory positions on Africa-focused investment vehicles.

The problem with the edifice he has built is that it is seemingly built almost entirely on omission, mischaracterisation, and exaggeration. The documents and testimony explored in this article are just a small fraction of the weight of evidence pointing unmistakably in this direction.

What he is, more than anything else, is a storyteller. He specialises in crafting readable, watchable, believable and engaging narratives.

The fact that he almost got sued by Jovago after a bitter departure? It is the French guy's fault. Allegedly running afoul of Polish mobsters while doing business back home? Poor, oppressed, serially targeted little Marek. It is not his fault that everybody wants a piece of him.

← **Tweet**

This Tweet is unavailable.

Seer.....ish
@nickleke

Replying to @marekchinedu

"@marekchinedu: It's official. Company I founded, Jovago, Wants to sue me. Why are you so stupid little french men?"

Zis iz Normal.

4:52 PM · Jan 31, 2016 · Twitter for Windows Phone

Showed off his Nigerian fiancee and declared her to a TEDx audience as the "love of his life" while allegedly on the run from a legal case in Nigeria, after which the relationship ended? No matter, he just moved on and got himself another African girlfriend.

Love Story

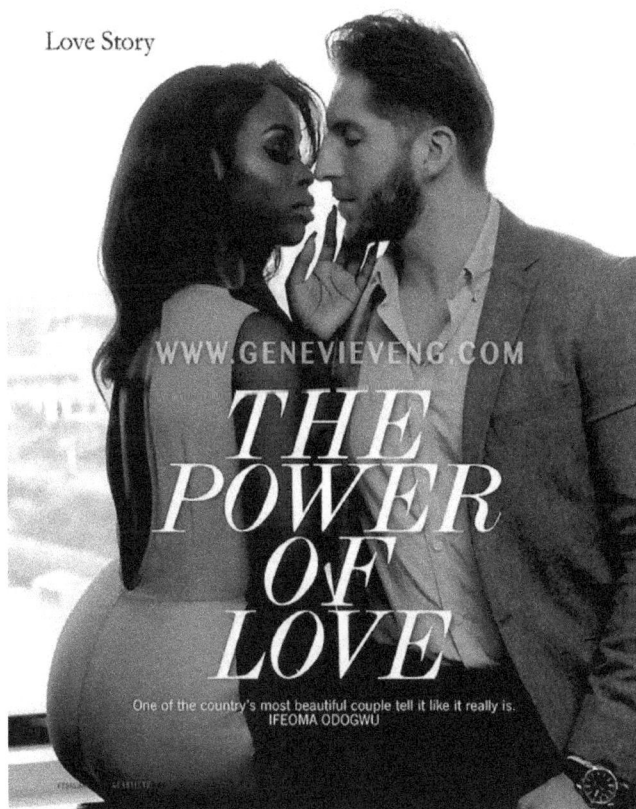

WWW.GENEVIEVENG.COM

THE POWER OF LOVE

One of the country's most beautiful couple tell it like it really is.
IFEOMA ODOGWU

"Built the Amazon of Africa?" Not even close to true. He was never on Jumia's management team and he was never a Jumia Co-Founder. He was actually the MD of a tiny Jumia division called Jovago which he left acrimoniously five months before it was collapsed into the Jumia brand. But that doesn't matter, because it's Marek. He'll put it on his LinkedIn profile anyway

Marek Zmysłowski
Entrepreneur, Investor, Advisor, Speaker, Bestselling Author

CEO & Founder
HotelOnline
Feb 2016 – Jan 2018 · 2 yrs
Lagos, Nigeria

Ridiculously simple booking and channel management tool helping hotels build online presence and maximize revenue.

https://www.tnooz.com/article/hoteloga-savanna-sunrise-merge/

Co-Founder and Managing Director
Jumia Travel
Mar 2013 – Feb 2016 · 3 yrs
Lagos, Nigeria

Jumia Travel (previously Jovago.com) - Africa's No.1 Hotel Booking Portal, backed by Rocket Internet, MTN and Millicom, listed on NYSE as part of Jumia Group.

Jovago.com TV Spot
2015: Looking for a...

techcabal   **Five months after leaving Jovago, Marek Zmyslowski has returned with HotelOga**

TC Daily
Reports
Events
Radar
Tech Women Lagos

He sees a story about the tragic murder of Gokada founder, Fahim Saleh? Before the corpse is even cold, he exploits the opportunity to use Saleh's death as a 'nudge wink' in the direction of alleged shady Nigerian investors. Only of course it turned out somewhat ironically that Fahim was actually murdered by someone who worked for him.

Marek Zmyslowski ✔ @marekchin... · 1h ⌄
How many more tech Founders need to die or disappear until we start looking at where the Investors got their money from. Tech is getting bigger, money amounts more serious, so the people behind it. Can we use dirty money for good things? That's an important moral question.

♡ 5   ⟳ 11   ♡ 16   ⬆

Keeps on claiming that he "won" his legal case in Nigeria? He did no such thing. He won an ancillary case against the famously efficient and process-driven Nigeria Police Force about procedural issues surrounding the freezing of his accounts. His substantive legal case in fact remains unresolved. He will of course never set foot in Nigeria to demonstrate that he has no outstanding legal issues here. Conveniently, this refusal will be "the godfather's" fault.

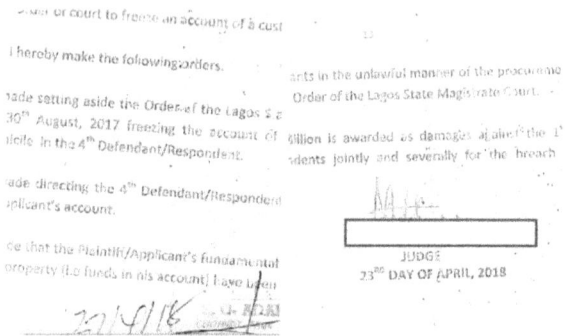

Marek Zmyslowski ✔ @marekchine... · 2h ∨
Nigerian Federal Court Judgment ruling illegality of my arrest warrant and bank account freeze. It's been more than a year. Nigeria has denied any explanations demanded by the Polish Ministry of Foreign Affairs.

Shopping his fictional account of events to Nigerian tech influencers so as to saturate the ecosystem with his story? That is Marek all over. He even pitched it to Edmund Olotu – the very same Edmund Olotu of Ferox Partners whom he allegedly stole from.

M Gmail

Fwd: I wrote a book "Chasing Black Unicorns. How building the Amazon of Africa put me on Interpol's Most Wanted list" and I want to give it to you for free.

Edmund Olotu ▮▮▮▮▮▮▮▮▮▮▮▮▮▮▮▮▮▮▮▮   Mon, Mar 30, 2020 at 7:29 PM
To: ▮▮▮▮▮▮▮▮▮▮▮▮▮▮▮▮▮▮▮▮
Cc: Guthel Kiron ▮▮▮▮▮▮▮▮▮▮▮▮▮▮▮

Is he going mad?? 😂 😂 😂

--------- Forwarded message ---------
From: **Marek Zmyslowski** <theookchinedu@gmail.com>
Date: Mon, Mar 30, 2020 at 7:26 PM
Subject: I wrote a book "Chasing Black Unicorns. How building the Amazon of Africa put me on Interpol's Most Wanted list" and I want to give it to you for free.
To: <edmund ▮▮▮▮▮▮▮▮▮▮▮

Hi there,

I hope you're doing well. You are a person of influence and I believe your positive opinion about the following topic will help a good cause. So let me explain why I wrote,
I've recently published the book "Chasing Black Unicorns. How building the Amazon of Africa put me on Interpol's Most Wanted list" and dedicated all of my income to impactful charity initiatives, such as MaYa Foundation. Read more about it here.

I would love to give you a free copy of my book.

All you need to do to receive it is to sign up for my newsletter. You can do it by clicking this link. Once you confirm your email address, you will get your voucher to redeem on the book site: www.chasingblackunicorns.com. Enjoy the read and don't forget to let me know what you think about it!

I have (like a typical straight white middle-aged male on self-quarantine) decided to share my take on the World - with the World, only once per week, I swear! I wrote for instance about:

Knowingly uses storytelling to sway public opinion and simultaneously sidestep and disrespect the Nigerian legal system? Again Marek all over.

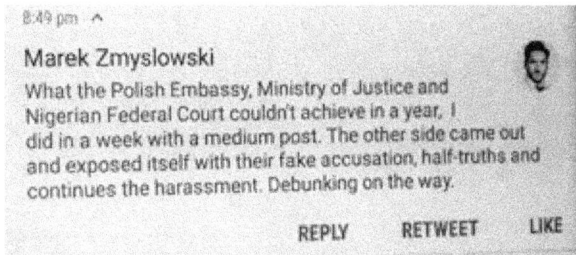

8:49 pm ⌃

Marek Zmyslowski
What the Polish Embassy, Ministry of Justice and Nigerian Federal Court couldn't achieve in a year, I did in a week with a medium post. The other side came out and exposed itself with their fake accusation, half-truths and continues the harassment. Debunking on the way.

REPLY   RETWEET   LIKE

Constantly talks himself up as a "bestselling author?" The book in question actually ranks at number 1,208,435 overall in the Amazon Kindle Store sales and does not make it into the top 100 by sales in any book category except "Amazon Brazil Travel Guides," which tells a story on its own.

Bestselling Author
Chasing Black Unicorns, The book
Oct 2019 – Present · 1 yr

Silicon Valley meets Indiana Jones – Chasing Black Unicorns is an autobiography written by Marek Zmysłowski, one of Poland's most respected internet entrepreneurs. Witty and humorous, the book covers many dramatic and often dangerous events. Before moving to Nigeria to set up the 'Amazon of Africa', Zmysłowski worked for one of Poland's biggest financial services companies, and is the founder of many online ventures in Central Europe. While establishing the first, online network of funeral services in Poland, he had to overcome challenges from criminal gangs running the market sector. His businesses in Nigeria have also made him enemies, powerful individuals who have corrupted police and government officials to stand against him. Overnight, Marek became an international fugitive and was put on the most wanted list by Interpol, an organization with a history of being manipulated by corrupt regimes. Zmysłowski describes this and many other events, putting them in the context of African history and cultures, a continent he is now deeply in love with.

All of the author's book profits support impactful charity initiatives in Africa.
see less

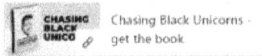

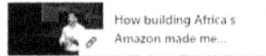

Chasing Black Unicorns -
get the book

How building Africa's
Amazon made me...

Product details

File Size : 1708 KB
Publisher : Schubert Media (September 24, 2019)
Publication Date : September 24, 2019
ASIN : B07YCT2N77
Print Length : 374 pages
Word Wise : Enabled
Language: : English
Page Numbers Source ISBN : 0578562472
Enhanced Typesetting : Enabled
Text-to-Speech : Not enabled
Screen Reader : Supported
X-Ray : Not Enabled
Lending : Enabled
Best Sellers Rank: #1,208,435 in Kindle Store (See Top 100 in Kindle Store)
#88 in Amazon Brazil Travel Guides
#190 in E-Commerce (Kindle Store)
#609 in African Travel

Somehow, using a mixture of the real privilege his white skin bestows on him in Africa, his storytelling abilities and sheer, razor sharp audacity, Marek Zmyslowski has managed to dazzle his way through a 7-year African tech career, failing his way up into board and advisory positions at some of the continent's most important tech and investment organisations. Anyone who is familiar with the story of the American missionary Renee Bach who showed up in Uganda and killed 105 people by pretending to be a doctor, will immediately notice the alarming similarities between both stories.

It is a depressingly familiar story – the white saviour from Ohio or Koszalin who waltzes into Africa to cosplay a Mathew McConaughey movie role, then successfully bullshits their way through the system and becomes genuinely powerful and dangerous – simply because nobody thought to **check** if anything they said is actually true. That is how this guy:

03/05/2006

Has conned the world into seeing him as this guy:

Source: Marekzmyslowski.com

Unfortunately, there is absolutely nothing there. Nothing that is, except a good story.

Gulbet Kiros sums up his damning opinion of Marek Zmyslowski in these words:

Overall, Marek is an opportunist and a delusional grifter with a penchant for publicity and self-promotion. When I see his public declarations, I genuinely question if his sense of reality is that far detached from the one the rest of us experience.

hotel oga investor and advisor, gulbet kiros

NOTE: This reporter reached out to Marek Zmyslowski for a statement, and we will publish an update to the story when he responds.

VIII

UNMASKING A JIHADI MASQUERADE:
THE MANY FACES OF
ISA ALI IBRAHIM PANTAMI

It is no longer a conspiracy theory. There is now hard evidence.

Nigerian Minister of Communications and Digital Economy, Ali Isa Ibrahim Pantami is a man of many descriptions. To some, he is a bright-eyed, relentlessly intelligent and academically competent Young Turk, who has found his way into the topmost level of Nigeria's government at the relatively young age of 48.

To others, he is a symbol of how deeply held and unapologetically public religious faith can coexist and interoperates with modernity and cosmopolitanism without contradiction.

His Twitter handle proudly displays his impressive academic credentials side-by-side with his proud

165

elementary educational background at an Islamic Tsangaya (non-Hausa readers might be more familiar with the term 'Almajiri').

Despite his impressive credentials and his reportedly genial personality which have endeared him to many however, several whispers and rumours about an allegedly dark past have continuously swirled around him at every point in his 5 year-old career as a public servant. From his 2016 appointment as DG/CEO at the National Information Technology Development Agency (NITDA), through to his appointment as a cabinet minister in 2019, these rumours have refused to go away.

Today for the first time ever, we can authoritatively lift the veil on Dr. Ali Isa Ibrahim Pantami and establish his strong and indisputable connections to - and deeply held sympathies for - the dark world of Salafist Islamic terrorism. It is a story that starts in Pantami Ward in Gombe State; meanders through extreme controversy at Abubakar Tafawa Balewa University in Bauchi State; takes a notable detour through a Saudi Arabian university known as a global hotbed for Salafist terror recruitment; and eventually ends with a known terror sympathiser and ideological 'gradualist' sitting in Nigeria's federal cabinet.

Pantami's Educational Controversies

Variously known as "Dr Isa Pantami," "Sheikh Ali Ibrahim," and "Shaykh Isa Ali Pantami" he has the unique distinction of being one of the very few people to achieve very high levels of academic achievement in both Western and Islamic education. Following a non-standard education path that included 4 years at a Tsangaya and 2 years of independent Islamic study after primary and secondary school, Pantami gained admission to the Abubakar Tafawa Balewa University (ATBU) in the late 1990s where he studied Computer Science. He graduated with a B.Tech. in 2003, followed by an M.Sc. in 2008 and this is where the story gets interesting.

His official Twitter handle includes a bio link to his Wikipedia page, which is poorly referenced and light on detail. On further examination of the sources attributed on his Wikipedia page, it becomes evident that much of what is written there was in fact lifted word-for-word from an official government press release sent out to the media.

∧ Early life and education ✎

Isa Ali Ibrahim (Pantami) was a Fulani, born on 20 October 1972 in Pantami Ward, Gombe State, Nigeria.[3][4] His mother was Hajiya Amina Umar Aliyu and his father was Alhaji Ali Ibrahim Pantami.[5] He started his education by attending traditional School for memorizing the Qur'an, called "Tsangaya School.[5]" He spent more than four years in the school. He later joined primary school in Pantami. He attended Government Science Secondary School in Gombe. After his secondary education, he spent additional two years seeking for more religious knowledge before moving to university. He studied Computer Science at Abubakar Tafawa Balewa University in Bauchi, Nigeria, gaining a BTech in 2003 Session and an MSc in 2008,[5][6][7] before obtaining a PhD from Robert Gordon University, Aberdeen, Scotland.[7] He spent his life pursuing both formal and informal education. by switching from one form to another.

He is also trained on Digital transformation in Harvard University, USA, then Management Strategy in both, Massachusetts Institute of Technology, and Institute of Management Development in Loussaune, Switzerland.[8] He was also in Cambridge University for Management Programme, among others.[9]

Isa Pantami's page on Wikipedia

Ali Isa Pantami

Ali Isa Pantami

Ibrahim Pantami was born on 20 October 1972 in Gombe State, Nigeria. He started his education by attending traditional School for memorizing the Qur'an, called "Tsangaya School." He spent more than four years in the school. He later joined primary school in Pantami. He attended Government Science Secondary School in Gombe. After his secondary education, he spent additional two years seeking for more religious knowledge before moving to university. He studied Computer Science at Abubakar Tafawa Balewa University in Bauchi, Nigeria, gaining a BTech in 2003 Session and an MSc in 2008, before obtaining a PhD from Robert Gordon University, Aberdeen, Scotland. He spent his life pursuing both formal and informal education, by switching from one form to another.

He is also trained on Digital transformation in Harvard University, USA, then Management Strategy in both, Massachusetts Institute of Technology, and Institute of Management Development in Loussaune, Switzerland. He was also in Cambridge University for Management Programme, among others.

Source article from PM News

Both straightforward accounts of his educational career make no mention of any controversy during his academic career. Keep this in mind for later. While digging into his academic qualifications, I was able to confirm that he did in fact obtain a PhD in 2014 from Robert Gordon University in Aberdeen. It was impossible to verify his claims of attending Harvard, MIT, IMD Lausanne and Oxford University independently, although the nature of short certificate programs makes it necessary to extend the benefit of the doubt. We can assume these claims are all true.

The neat cover story starts to fall apart however, when a reference from a U.S. diplomatic cable leaked in 2009 by Wikileaks suggests that in his prior iteration as an academic at ATBU, Pantami was in fact a radical extremist cleric whose views were so repulsive that he was kicked out of the university and from a mosque in his native Gombe State.

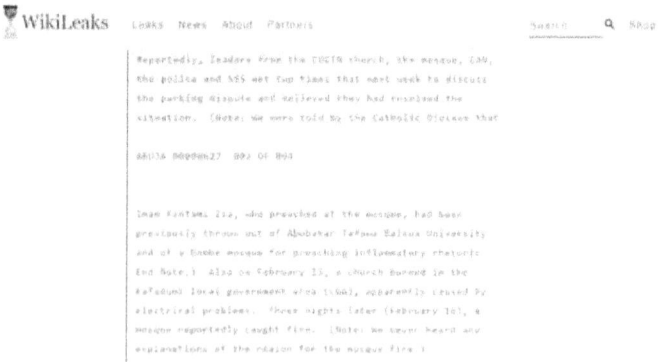

It gets more interesting.

Where his personally-approved Wikipedia profile makes no mention of a stint in Saudi Arabia or what happened there, a bit of digging turns up information that significantly changes the clean-cut picture he is eager to present. According to multiple verifiable online and offline sources, Isa Pantami in fact spent a number of years learning and lecturing at the University of Medina in Saudi Arabia.

Isa Ali Pantami's Profile on IslamicMarkets.com

This information is very important for two reasons. First, the Islamic University of Medina (IUM) is globally recognised as a hotspot for Salafist Islamic terror recruitment. While it does not itself teach or openly condone terror, it is the undisputed global headquarters of Salafist fundamentalism. The below excerpts from a UK Guardian article from 2001 illustrates how IUM serves as a recruitment pipeline that feeds extremist groups like the Taliban and Al-Qaeda.

Investigators hunting members of Osama bin Laden's network have discovered that all the suspected terrorists arrested in Europe over the past 10 months follow an extreme Salafi interpretation of Islam, according to a source close to the investigation and a detailed intelligence assessment seen by the Guardian.

A document found by the FBI in the luggage of one of the September 11 hijackers also suggests Salafi influence. Salafis not only take the Koran literally but seek to revert to an ancient and "pure" form of Islam. Although most are ultra-conservative, there is a militant wing to which Bin Laden and his followers belong.

The link between Salafis and Bin Laden's terrorist web will prove acutely embarrassing to Saudi Arabia, whose royal family has invested huge sums in spreading Salafi thought abroad. The leading centre for the study and export of Salafi ideas is the Islamic University of Medina, in Saudi Arabia, which was founded by the king in 1961 "to convey the eternal message of Islam to the entire world".

Investigators in at least nine European countries working against the clock to track down suspected members of cells sponsored by al-Qaida have found a Salafi connection in every case.

> The Islamic University of Medina has long been known as a recruiting ground for fighters, despite periodic clampdowns. Formal teaching is of the ultra-conservative kind approved by the Saudi royals but the problem is what happens outside the classrooms, according to former students.

Ibrahim (not his real name) is a British Muslim who attended the university. "It has to be seen to be promoting orthodox Islam," he said. "But there's a lot of shoulder-rubbing and people go on to develop their own ideas. Students meet people who speak with passion and fire, and eat squatting on mud floors."

For some, this has a radicalising effect as they become aware of a huge contradiction between the simple lives of the early Muslims and those of the Saudi elite who sponsor the university. Another problem, a former diplomat in Saudi Arabia says, is that many of Medina's graduates are virtually unemployable except as religious teachers. "Some can't find jobs and drift into Bin Laden circles."

Source: The Guardian

The second reason that we should be very interested in Pantami's undisclosed sojourn within the world of Islamic education is that according to multiple sources, he studied the teachings of hardline Salafist scholars including Sheikh Muhammad Saleh Al-Uthaymeen. For those who do not know Sheikh Al-Uthaymeen, here is a collection of quotes and fatwas issued by the man described as a "Giant of the Salafi movement."

The former Grand Mufti Abdel Aziz bin Baz had argued that lifting the ban would corrupt society with promiscuity and sin.

Senior council member, Saleh al-Fawzan, defended the ban, asserting that it would force women to take off their full-face veils to let them to see the road and allow them to leave the house at night.

Wahhabi giant Mohamed ibn al-Uthaymeen backed the ban because according to him driving would lead the free-mixing of men and women at traffic lights, petrol stations, police checkpoints as well as other car-related encounters.

One cleric even claimed that driving would damage women's ovaries and hurt their fertility.

Last week, a cleric who said women should not be allowed to drive because they have a "quarter" of the brainpower of men was banned from preaching.

Source: Al Araby

C-sections: 'anti-Islam plot'

But an edict from Islamic militants published in the northern Syrian province of Deir ez-Zor has ordered medics to not use the procedure, "In order to assist the believers from the sons of Islam who are working in the medical corps to support their brothers from the poor and others besides them from the Muslim populace, and with the desire to keep the course of medical work removed from arbitrary whim.

"This is to be considered as tantamount to a written order and all who contravene it will be held accountable in the Dar al-Qada [IS judiciary] with attendant consequence."

Sheikh Muhammad ibn Saalih al Uthaymeen (1925-2001), a prominent Sunni Muslim Islamic scholar, stated in a ruling on Islamic doctrine that Muslim mothers should not use pain-relieving medication during labour and delivery.

In a statement published on IslamQA website he said: "I would like to take this opportunity to point out a phenomenon that has been mentioned to us, which is that many obstetricians, male and female, in the hospitals are too keen for birth to take place by surgical means, which is known as a Caesarean.

"I am afraid that this may be a plot against the Muslims, because the more births take place in this manner, the more the skin of the abdomen is weakened and pregnancy becomes more dangerous for the woman, and she becomes unable to get pregnant."

Source: IBI Times

Q. Should a husband or wife stay in a marriage if their partner no longer prays?

* Fatwa from Sheikh Ibn al-Uthaymin (a prominent 20th-century Saudi scholar) By abandoning his or her prayers, a person leaves Islam. It is forbidden, therefore, for a Muslim to remain with a husband or a wife who no longer prays.

Q. Is free thought and faith a positive attribute?

* Sheikh Ibn al-Uthaymin Whoever argues that a person is entitled to complete freedom of faith is an unbeliever, guilty of the major sin of disbelief.

Source: UK Independent

Sheikh Al-Uthaymeen says that peace between Muslims and non-Muslims can only be temporary because "jihad is the highest form of Islam."

A transcription of the video above goes as follows:

"If someone was to say: Is a treaty permissible between us and the Mushrikeen (variously translated as disbelievers/idolaters/atheists), so that we don't fight them and they don't fight us? The answer is yes. If we need this, then it is allowed. For instance if the Muslims are in a state of weakness and they are not capable of fighting the enemy. So there is nothing wrong with carrying out a treaty between us and them. However, would the treaty have to be restricted to a limited time period or not?

We say the treaty is of three types: The first type is the restricted treaty meaning that we (the Muslims) say to the disbelievers, "Between us and you is ten years, or five years or eight years (of the treaty)."[…] The second type is the endless treaty which stipulates that we never attack. This is prohibited and I think it is by consensus because this necessitates abolishment of Jihad, and Jihad is the peak of Islam. There will be no power for a nation except by way of Jihad, if it is capable of this."

For good measure, Sheikh Al-Uthaymeen also specified that his definition of 'Mushikreen' (disbelievers/people without God) also includes Christians and Jews.

Question: One of the preachers in one of the mosques in Europe claimed that it is not allowed to consider Jews and Christians disbelievers. You know – may Allaah preserve you – that most of the people who attend the mosques in Europe have very little knowledge. We fear that statements like this one will become widespread. Therefore, we request from you a complete and clear answer to this question.

Answer: I say: The statement that came from that man is misguidance. In fact, it can be blasphemy. This is because Allaah has declared that Jews and Christians are disbelievers (kuffaar) in His Book. Allaah has said:

'And the Jews say, 'Ezra is the son of Allaah' and the Christians say, 'The Messiah is the son of Allaah.' This is a saying from their mouths. They imitate the saying of the disbelievers of old. Allaah's curse be on them, how they are deluded away from the truth. They took their rabbis and their monks as lords besides Allaah and [they also took as Lord] the Messiah, son of Mary. But they were commanded only to worship none but One God. Praise and Glory be to Him. [far above is He] from having the partners they associate with Him.' [at-Taubah 9:30-31]

That shows that they are polytheists who associate partners with Allaah. In other verses, Allaah has made it clear that they are disbelievers:

Source: Shaykh Ibn Uthaymeen, Fatawa Islamiya, vol. 1, p. 87, Darussalam Publishers

Just a Series of Coincidences?

So far, we have established that Isa Pantami has a side to his past educational pursuits that most people are not aware of. However, it is tempting to dismiss these links to Salafist terror and extremism as merely circumstantial. Apart from what is essentially gossip from a Wikileaks cable, the documented views of the teachers he studied with, and the well-earned terror-recruitment-hotspot reputation of the Islamic University of Medina where he taught, there is no actual evidence so far to suggest that Isa Pantami himself is an extremist. Right?

He himself has tried to present himself as the unfortunate victim of such circumstances beyond his control. Commenting on a recent viral video that depicted him in a debate with Boko Haram founder Mohammed Yusuf, he claimed that he was in fact a moderate Islamic scholar taking on the self-imposed and heroic task of de-radicalising Salafist extremists using his superior Islamic education and his ability to debate.

He is apparently the victim of bigotry perpetrated by people who do not understand Hausa or context. How on earth could a STEM PhD holder with academic achievements spanning Harvard, MIT, Oxford and Cambridge be a low-key Islamic extremist and terror apologist? What a ridiculous thought.

Or is it?

Cross Section of Isa Pantami's "Suwaye Yan Taliban" ("Who Are The Taliban?") Public Lecture

In his prior iteration as Imam Isa Ali Ibrahim Pantami, our hero has been accused of making several incendiary utterances and expressing support for violent jihadists around the world. With the exception of a Wikileaks cable, there has been precious little to substantiate these claims. Until now.

For the first time, readers can listen to Imam Isa Ali Ibrahim Pantami in his own words expressing deep support and admiration for Osama bin-Laden and the Afghan Taliban, even praying "May God help us to imitate their good." The following recording is from a public lecture Pantami delivered on September 12, 2006 in Bauchi State, titled "Suwaye Yan Taliban" ("Who Are The Taliban"). The recording is also freely available on the Nigerian Islamic community website *DawahNigeria. com.*

The following translation was made by Andrea Brigaglia PhD, Director of the Centre for Contemporary Islam at the University of Cape Town, South Africa. It can be found in her 2019 paper "Debating Boko Haram."

Osama Bin Laden is mentioned in various instances in this section, with his name always followed by the formula haẓahu 'Llāh (may God preserve him). At the same time, however, the government of Saudi Arabia is also the object of unreserved praises, being described

177

as "our qibla" and "the original abode of faith." The author mentions the Saudi and Pakistani involvement in the Afghani conflict as starting only after the end of the Afghani war, in a section titled "the post-Soviet era." It was the leadership of the Arab mujāhidīn, Pantami continues, who invited Muslim countries such as Saudi Arabia and Pakistan to be involved in the post-war peace agreement, and not Saudi Arabia and Pakistan who, in coordination with the United States, had funded the mujāhidīn for years.

References are made to a meeting held between all the leaders of the Afghani factions in Medina, with quotes from a book authored by the Saudi scholar Mūsā al-Qarnī, who is one of Pantami's main sources (and who would later, in 2011, be handed a 20-year prison term by the Saudi government). Similarly, the anarchy that followed the end of the anti-Soviet war in Afghanistan is not attributed by Pantami to the contrasting agendas of the various political actors involved (the Afghani factions, the US, Pakistan, Saudi Arabia, and the Arab foreign fighters), but to the "divide and rule" policy of the kuffār (unbelievers).

[Pantami then says that] it was in response to this anarchy that "The Commander of the Believers, Mullah Mohammad Omar, may God preserve him," entered the scene. The formation of the Taliban, on 1st Muharram 1415, corresponding to 24 June 1994, is reconstructed through accurate historical detail fused with some hagiographic data: the 313 scholars who first established the Taliban, for example, correspond to the 313 companions who fought the Battle of Badr (624) alongside the Prophet. The ultimate goal of the Taliban was to bring peace and reconciliation in Afghanistan by "establishing an Islamic leadership, a Caliphate and the Sharia, as every Muslim is commanded to do."

Here Pantami relies not only on the book by al-Qarnī but also on 'The Rise of the Taliban' and on a book by the Nigerian Salisu Shehu, 'Who are the Talibans'. Pantami [says] that the Taliban are not immune from error. His particular concern is that "about 5% of them" have a penchant for Sufism, which obviously is, in his eyes, an imperfection in their credentials. The remaining 95%, however, are rooted in the "purest Sunni doctrine" (tataccen aƙidar Sunna): "they are people raised in the religious way, may God enable us to imitate their good" mutane masu tarbiya ta addini, Allah ya ba mu ikon koyi da alheransu). In particular, Pantami says that the Taliban are to be praised and imitated in three respects.

The first is the destruction of the two "idols of the Buddha" at Bamiyan. In imitating them, the Nigerian Muslims should long for the day in which every "idolatrous image" will be erased from the Nigerian currency, and no picture will be used on passports and electoral posters, for photos and images are contrary to the Sharia. The second is their effort to impose a strict adherence to the Sunna in the dress code of Afghani women (full face-veiling) and men (st-long beard and trousers cut at the length of the ankle). The third is the protection offered to Osama Bin Laden after the Americans rushed to accuse him of being responsible for the events of 9/11, by arguing that not only was there insufficient proof of his involvement, but also that "even if he had done it, according to the Sharia he should not be handed to you."

The section concludes with a quote from Safar al-Hawali which is also a favourite scare-quote in the reservoir of contemporary islamophobes, according to which "hating America is part of our creed." This is followed by prayers for the success of the Taliban; new comparisons between the Taliban and the Prophet's Companions; and prayers for Bin Baz, al-Albani, Ibn al-'Uthayimin and Azzam. Finally, there is an invitation to learn from the Taliban's experience by studying hard "medicine and engineering" while patiently preparing for the moment when Nigeria will be ripe for a leader of the stature of Mullah Omar.

The first questioner asks how one should respond to those Salafis who reject Osama Bin Laden because of his killing of innocent unbelievers; this is probably a reference to the quietist and Saudi-loyalist strand of Salafi thought in Nigeria, represented by scholars such as Muhammad Sani Umar Rijiyar Lemo.

Pantami responded to the questioner by saying that yes, these scholars have some truth, for Bin Laden is liable to make mistakes, but "I still consider him as a better Muslim than myself." "We are all happy whenever unbelievers are being killed," continued Pantami, "but the Sharia does not allow us to kill them without a reason." "Our zeal (hamasa) should not take precedence over our obedience to the sacred law."

The second questioner asks how a jihad could take place in Nigeria when there is no consensus over a leader, in contrast to the consensus that (if one has to believe to the lecture) existed in Afghanistan around the gure of Mullah Omar. Pantami answers that this was precisely the goal of his lecture; in other words, to point out the need to establish in Nigeria an overall Islamic leadership similar to Mullah Omar's, before moving to the next step.

In Nigeria, continued Pantami (emphasis added), this is the time for correction (gyara) and preparation (isti'dād): "How can you start a jihad, when your father is still going around without a beard? When your mother is still going around with a mere transparent veil (gyale) rather than with a full-length hijab?

"Any effort to start a jihad without having established correct Islamic practices is doomed to failure, and this is precisely the main lesson to draw from the Afghan Taliban, whose success was established upon their unwavering attachment to the Sunna. This is the reason, concludes Pantami with a new reference to the "Kanamma affair" and to his critical engagement with Yusuf, why "any attempt to start a struggle that you have seen me rejecting so far, [it was because] it was not led by scholars and there was no understanding of the Sunna." Thus the second question, focused on the possible implementation of jihad in Nigeria, was answered with a call for postponement (irjā', Yusuf would say).

The third questioner asks how to make sense of the alliance between Saudi Arabia and the western countries fighting Al-Qaeda, such as the United Kingdom and the

United States. Unfortunately, the recording stops before one can listen to Pantami's answer.

Isa Pantami - A Jihadi Gradualist in Sheep's Clothing

According to a 2017 paper published by the US Institute of Peace and the Wilson Centre, Al Qaeda's jihadi tactics have morphed over the years from "shock and awe" events like September 11 to a strategy known as "gradualism." Explaining the subtle difference between open terrorism and gradualist terrorism, the paper says:

"ISIS is a political extremist actor, while al-Qaeda has become an extremist political actor. In other words, ISIS is more of an extremist movement with political goals. ISIS is unwilling to compromise; its behaviour is unlikely to change whatever the incentives. In contrast, al-Qaeda is now more of a political organisation with extremist beliefs, although that does not mean it can be co-opted. Both ISIS and al-Qaeda have long-term strategies to create a Salafist utopia. ISIS's core strategy is to pursue a Salafi state through continuous confrontations both within Muslim-dominated countries and outside them. ISIS believes Muslims can be held to an interpretation of Sharia today.

[…] Al-Qaeda's strategy is more gradualist. It believes that Muslims must be educated first on Sharia, that the idea of jihad must be popularised, and that

Muslims must be convinced to take up arms as the only method of emancipation. It is less exclusionary. It has forged alliances and quietly entrenched itself and its ideas within local communities with the aim of eventually building a pure salafi one."

The irrefutable evidence of Isa Pantami's own pronouncements, hitherto hidden behind what he considered to be the veil of the Hausa and Arabic language tells a very clear story about exactly who Isa Ali Ibrahim Pantami is, and what his existential goals are. It is no longer a conspiracy theory. There is now hard evidence.

At this point, the only course of action left is for President Muhammadu Buhari to quickly and unceremoniously fire Dr. Pantami from his sensitive job where he sits on the National Executive Council and has access to the personal data of tens of millions of Nigerians. Nigeria can definitely do better than have an openly self-proclaimed Al-Qaeda sympathiser as its Minister of Communications and Digital Economy.

NB: In the few hours between announcing that I would publish this story and when it went live, my Google account was hacked, and an unknown entity tried to hijack control of the working document I used to draft this story.

I have reached out to Isa Pantami for his comment, if any, on the story.

IX

ISA ALI PANTAMI – THE INSIDE STORY OF NIGERIA'S MINISTER OF COMMUNICATIONS & DIGITAL ECONOMY

Minister of Communications and Digital Economy, Dr. Isa Ali Ibrahim Pantami is the proverbial chameleon with one eye on the past and one eye on the future. Depending on the situation or who is involved in it, he sometimes comes across as a cosmopolitan technocrat with a strong academic background. At other times, he transforms into a knuckle-dragging troglodyte spewing forth parochial religious and micro-ethnic sentiments.

Perhaps because of the sheer disconnect between the different Isa Pantamis known to different people, it has always been difficult to conclusively nail him down to a singular identity. To those who work around him or watch him on television delivering speeches about Nigeria's broadband masterplan in his trademark reedy voice, it can be very disorienting to process the idea that this slightly built man with the gold-rimmed prescription glasses could be one of the most dangerous men in Nigeria right now.

Even after extensively-researched exposes about the furious and unrepentant religious extremist that resides somewhere within Isa Pantami's polite exterior, it is simply difficult for many to accept. How is it possible that this man with a PhD from Aberdeen and several certificate programs at the world's most prestigious institutions is also a supporter of Al-Qaeda and the Taliban, as well as an instigator of deadly religious crises in Northern Nigeria?

After reading Sheikh Pantami's mealy-mouthed attempt to distance himself from his own utterances during a Ramadan service on Saturday April 17, 2021, I decided that the best way to break through his manufactured genteel posturing and lift the veil of denial is not to write another extensively-sourced 2,000-word deep dive, but rather to let Pantami himself do the work for us.

Pro-Terrorist Rhetoric and a Buhari Cameo

The man who would later become "Sheikh," "Imam," "Mallam" and "Dr," Isa Pantami was born on October 20, 1972 in the Pantami Ward of Gombe State. Pantami Ward is noted for being the last holdout of the infamous

Maitatsine Islamic uprisings of the 1980s. Some have argued that these uprisings were in fact precursors to the Boko Haram crisis that would follow 2 decades later.

It is impossible to verify whether the adolescent Pantami was ideologically influenced by the Maitatsine-type Islamic cult which grew in Pantami Ward and culminated in a bloody showdown with authorities on April 29, 1985. What we do know for sure about Pantami is that after graduating in 2003 from the Abubakar Tafawa Balewa University (ATBU) in Bauchi with a B.Tech. in Computer Science, he became the Chief Imam at ATBU and an influential public figure in Bauchi.

On September 12, 2006, roughly one month shy of his 34th birthday, Pantami delivered a now-infamous public lecture in Bauchi titled "Suwaye Yan Taliban" ("Who Arc The Taliban?). This was just one of several incendiary sermons and public lectures that Imam Pantami delivered over the course of nearly a decade in Bauchi, but the reason it has now become infamous is because it found its way onto the internet. First Italian academic Dr. Andrea Brigaglia of the University of Cape Town Centre for Contemporary Islam published a paper in 2019 with a translation of the question-and-answer segment of 'Suwaye Yan Taliban.' Then a 54-minute audio recording of the lecture mysteriously turned up on a Nigerian Islamic community website.

'Suwaye Yan Taliban' on Dawah Nigeria

By luck or by design, 'Suwaye Yan Taliban' has now become the proverbial bone stuck in Isa Pantami's throat. At first he denied making such pronouncements outright. Then when the audio recording with his unmistakable voice showed up, he claimed that Dr. Brigaglia's translation was inaccurate, suggesting that whoever translated it either did not understand Hausa properly, or simply did not like him. Several influential friends of the house eagerly went to work with this narrative, attempting to take advantage of the fact that most Nigerians who have a keen interest in this story are not (native) Hausa speakers.

To establish whether there was any truth in this narrative, I collaborated with a trusted contact who was born and raised in northern Nigeria and is a native Hausa speaker. Passing across the 54-minute audio recording, I tasked him with extracting 4 parts of the recording that confirm or refute Brigaglia's translation of what Pantami said 15 years ago. For the first time since the story broke, I can present 4 accurately translated and carefully subtitled extracts from 'Suwaye Yan Taliban' that tell a very clear story about who 33 year-old Isa Pantami was.

In the first extract below, Pantami describes the Afghan Taliban in glowing terms, saying that they have undergone "trials from Allah" while dealing with kafuri ("infidels") from the Western world who wish to destroy the "good image" of the Taliban.

The transcript for the segment above, taken from 2:50 – 3:57 of the full recording reads:

"With respect to enquiries/clarification on this topic, I decided to respond timely so as to underscore the importance of the Topic to the people. A very important thought that came into my mind, is that what our brethren-Al Sunnah (Salafists) want to know is how the Talibans who lived in Afghanistan were subjected to trials from Allah on this earth. Subjected to a test of faith and love.

Furthermore, there were a group of people, Infidels, from the Western World, who don't have any other target in this life except to destroy the good image of the Talibans in the eyes of their Muslim brethren, to destroy the Taliban image even in the eyes of the Infidels themselves, by means of accusing the Taliban of deeds which were not committed by them.

The next extract is taken from 13:14 – 15:19 of the full recording.

"The Land of Afghanistan was in a terrible state until the Monarchy was abolished, that is Kingship System, exactly around 1978 Christian Era. If you did arithmetic, you'd notice that about 30 years had gone by. Afghanistan found itself in a state of anarchy to the extent that the infidels began to plan on coming in and dominating Afghanistan. This is because when you are religiously pious, patient, worshipping God, reading the Quran, our adversaries- the Infidels, especially the United States of America are always distressed. As such, they are always lurking around and looking for an opportunity at launching an attack against you. Right now, they are claiming to be super powers, whereas the USSR was formerly the World Power.

Under the pretext of promoting peace, The USA invaded Afghanistan. Their entry into the country was characterised by their support for one group against the other. Right now, if Allah were to bring a test of faith on Nigeria, who do you think would be the first to invade Nigeria? AMERICA! If they invaded, who do you think they would support? Muslims or Infidels? INFIDELS! This is exactly how they seek to operate. This is the reason why in the rules of Islam, it is wrong to take premature action without making Preparation (Istidhad). This is the path of God's Religion."

Apart from Pantami's repeated use of the word "kafuri" (infidel) to refer to non-Muslims, the important thing to note about this extract is that the inference in the second paragraph is that not only are Muslims at war with the USA by default, but that the only reason they should not "take action", i.e. a violent jihad is that if the USA intervened, it would side with non-Muslims. This is an important point because it ties closely with the "gradualist" philosophy propagated by Al-Qaeda, whereby emphasis is placed on preparation, typically through political means, instead of simple confrontation favoured by the likes of ISIS and Boko Haram.

In the next segment taken from 17:28 – 17:51, Pantami makes a nudge-wink reference to "Mr. Zero Zero" (a northern Nigerian reference to Rt. Gen Muhammadu Buhari) being a "true Muslim" and hence his preferred candidate in the upcoming (2007) elections.

"They have a plan of invading and dominating Afghanistan, so as to impose whatever they like on its Government. All along, this is their strategy all over the World, where any Nation of Infidels that is powerful can impose themselves on any other country. This is why we have been praying to Almighty Allah to urgently bring Mr Zero-Zero to Power in Nigeria. May Almighty Allah give us a true Muslim who fears Almighty Allah. I'm sure that you all know who I'm referring to, I don't need to elaborate."

[Audience responds]: "Yes!"

For reference, the main candidates in the 2007 general election were Umaru Musa Yar'adua (PDP), Muhammadu Buhari (ANPP) and Atiku Abubakar (AC). Yar'adua eventually won with 24.6 million votes to Buhari's 6 million votes and Atiku's 2.6 million votes. This is the first clue in the story of Isa Pantami that hints at a longstanding relationship with Nigeria's current president. •

The fourth and final extract taken from 52:35 – 53:21 contains a chilling set of prayers that directly instigate Pantami's audience against the Nigerian state in a manner not dissimilar to that of Boko Haram founder Mohammed Yusuf.

"And therefore, we are praying to God that based on our understanding we pray for a day when the images on the notes in our pockets will be removed. No Muslim Cleric has ever spoken against these images as forbidden. May we be self-sufficient enough not to need this currency. It is against the religion to put even the images of the Companions of the Prophet on the currency. May Allah help us to see that day when the Gregorian date, the Calendar of the Infidels that is on the notes is removed. And that day is coming when it will certainly be removed."

A Case Study in Dissembling, Dishonesty and Disingenuousness

Since the audio recording emerged, making it difficult to deny and obfuscate any longer, Pantami has changed tack. In a Q&A segment during his daily Ramadan lecture at Annor Mosque in Abuja on Saturday April 17, 2021, Pantami said:

> "*Some of the comments I made some years ago that are generating controversies now were based on my understanding of religious issues at the time, and I have changed several positions taken in the past based on new evidence and maturity.*
>
> *I was young when I made some of the comments; I was in university, some of the comments were made when I was a teenager. I started preaching when I was 13, many scholars and individuals did not understand some of international events and therefore took some positions based on their understanding, some have come to change their positions later*"
>
> *– Isa Pantami responding to questions about his jihadist preachings*

This statement is important because it shows that Pantami relies of the credulity and lack of research of his audience to get away with his everlasting chameleon act of constant reinvention without accountability. Pantami is clearly expecting his audience to take to heart the emotionally believable tale of a "teenager" or "13 year-old" being "immature" and misled. In fact, "Suwaye Yan Taliban' was delivered in 2006 when Pantami was 33 – 14 years older than the oldest possible teenager.

Understanding this type of dishonesty is central to unraveling the Isa Pantami myth and lifting the layers of carefully constructed falsehoods and misdirection that one of Nigeria's most dangerous individuals uses to conceal himself. Here is another example of Pantami being disingenuous, this time in response to a question about his ouster as Chief Imam at ATBU:

DR. ISA ALI PANTAMI: Cleric, Scholar, Teacher, Academic, Nigeria's Minister of Communications and Digital Economy

"
While I was doing that, many students were dismissed from the university. I attended Government Secondary School, Gombe. During my studies, some were dismissed because of extremism. I was not one of them. In Abubakar Tafawa Balewa University, I was not dismissed, but during my stay, many were dismissed. In fact, when I graduated, my university even asked me to come back and lecture there.

Dr. Isa Ali Pantami

"

A solid answer to a question nobody asked.

Reading this answer, you would think that Pantami has directly denied the story referenced in a 2009 Wikileaks cable about his unceremonious ouster from ATBU. In fact however, he has cleverly danced around the question which was "Were you thrown out as Chief Imam at ATBU after formenting a series of religious crises in the community?" Instead he provided an answer to "Were you thrown out of ATBU as a student?" A fine answer it was – but not an answer to the question. He fully expects his audience to lack the mental rigour to spot this obvious disingenuousness, which enables him to escape being pinned down on anything.

When all else fails, the second tactic Pantami employs is to issue vigorous, bloviating denials, often lying through his teeth. An example of this is his May 2020 fallout with NIDCOM Chair, Abike Dabiri-Erewa, where armed men acting on his orders forcefully evicted her and her staff from their office at the NCC. While Dabiri-Erewa was very clear and forthright about what happened, with several eyewitnesses corroborating her account of events, Pantami had this to say:

A clear parallel can be drawn with his recent reaction to stories about his presence on a US terror watch list. Of course he knew better than anyone that with the record he has and the extensive intelligence network operated by the NSA, CIA and FBI, it is almost impossible for someone like him to not be on such a watch list. For that matter, he also knew that it was impossible to fact check such a story because the intelligence agencies involved will never voluntarily divulge such information. Yet here he was in true bloviating Pantami fashion – strutting for his audience and basking in a phantom win before completely reversing himself a few days later and claiming that it was all the fault of his misguided teenage self.

"I'm not that person anymore" –

Most blatantly of all, Pantami's declaration that he no longer agrees with his jihadi iteration from 2006 is demonstrably false, and this can be easily proven. Here is just one example. On March 22, 2021, Pantami's Federal Ministry of Communications and Digital Economy hosted a virtual flag-off ceremony for a capacity development programme empowering 600 people with VSAT Installation Skills. Pantami himself was in attendance and he spoke at the event.

This would all seem very run-of-the-mill and prosaic until you click on the YouTube link in the tweet. Was it livestreamed by the FMCoDE's YouTube channel? No. Was it livestreamed by the NTA YouTube channel? No. Channels TV? No. TVC? No. AIT? No. No major broadcaster was engaged to livestream this event hosted by Pantami's Ministry. Instead, a little-known Islamic TV channel called Al-Afrikiy was contracted to relay an event organised by the Federal Government of Nigeria.

It is important to point out that Al-Afrikiy is not merely an Islamic-influenced, or Islamic-leaning TV station which also covers other things. Al-Afrikiy is an

Islam-only TV channel. It broadcasts strictly religious content. Getting this channel to host an FMCoDE event would be the equivalent of getting TB Joshua's Emmanuel TV to host an official Federal Government event.

An islam-only TV channel somehow got to host Pantami's fmcode event

It gets worse.

Al-Afrikiy is not just an Islam-only TV channel. Its social media handles also get involved in religious controversies, as proven by this post from its Facebook page.

✏ Author
Al-Afrikiy Islamic Television
A seasoned journalist, Brother Ismail Omipidan wrote this fantastic piece on his Facebook page

CAN, Religion and NASS leadership
By Ismail Omipidan

I don't like introducing religion into issues that are purely political and which require only political solution to get them resolved. Reason: Most people who argue purely from religious point of view are too emotional and sometimes irrational. Thus, their arguments, most often become illogical.

But I feel compelled to make this intervention because even some journalists who have reported the National Assembly over the years and who should know better appear to have failed in their primary responsibility of providing the Christian Association of Nigeria (CAN) with the correct information. If they do, CAN would probably not have come up with the letter to our lawmakers requesting that either the president of the Senate or Speaker of the House of Representatives should be a Christian.

I had in one of my posts about five days ago stated

This is the sort of outfit hired to broadcast FG events now apparently

A look through Al-Afrikiy's YouTube uploads shows that this channel uploads exclusively religious content, with only 2 exceptions. The 2 of them have something in common which readers will immediately spot.

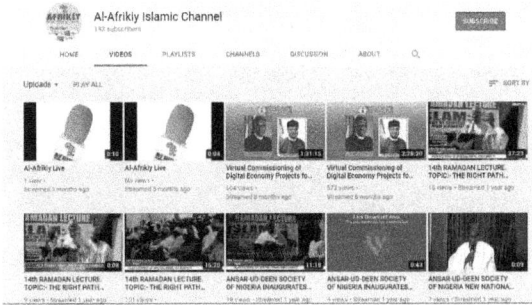

Notice anything?

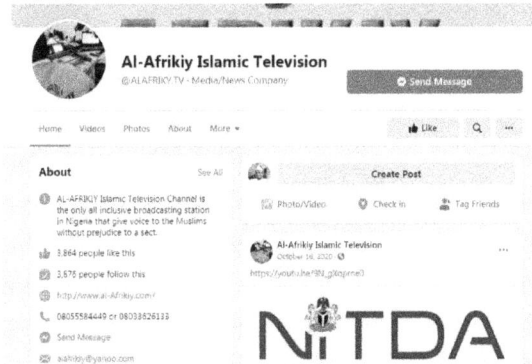

Here too…

But wait. It gets even worse.

I looked up the website link on Al-Afrikiy's Facebook page. I wanted to get a sense for what kind of no-name religion-only channel somehow gets the inside track on broadcasting events by a federal ministry – a contract that I know for a fact actual TV broadcasters would bite off Pantami's hand for. This was what I saw:

Pantami's "Federal Ministry of Communications and Digital Economy" has its events relayed by an unknown Islamic TV station without a functioning website.

I rest my case here.

X

MURDER IN UYO:
WHO KILLED HINY UMOREN?

On Friday April 29, a 26 year-old lady set out around 1PM to attend a job interview in Uyo, Akwa Ibom State. Having recently completed her university program despite losing both parents, she was looking for a way to support herself before being called up for the National Youth Service Corps (NYSC) program.

Instead of a job interview and hope for the future however, what she would actually encounter on that day would become one of the most shocking stories to ever emerge from Nigeria.

Iniobong "Hiny" Umoren became the subject of a desperate nationwide search led by Nigerian Twitter users after her friend Umoh Uduak put out an urgent appeal. She was eventually found, but unfortunately the worst had already happened. The police would later confirm that she was found dead, having been raped, murdered and then buried in a shallow grave.

In the wake of a crowdsourced social media sleuthing campaign which uncovered his identity, a primary suspect Frank Uduak Ezekiel Akpan was also arrested.

In a manner completely uncharacteristic of Nigeria's elephant-paced justice system, the Akwa Ibom State Police Command rapidly announced that it had extracted a confession from Akpan, and even identified his motive – he was a serial rapist and serial killer acting alone. End of story and job done.

"On 30/04/2021, the Command received a report on the disappearance of the victim.

"Following available leads, men of the Anti-Kidnapping Squad of the Command, led by CSP Inengiye Igosi, consolidated on the initial great progress made by the DPO Uruan, SP Samuel Ezeugo and arrested the perpetrator who confessed to have lured his victim to his house in the guise of giving her a job, but ended up sexually and physically assaulting her which led to her death.

"To cover his tracks, he dragged and buried her in a shallow grave in his father's compound," Mr MacDon, a superintendent of police, said in the statement.

The body of the woman has been exhumed and deposited at the University of Uyo Teaching Hospital, Uyo, the police said.

"Suspect is a confessed serial rapist who has owned up to the raping of other victims.

Police statement on Hiny Umoren case

Naturally, this neat explanation did not satisfy many, who felt that Akpan could not have acted alone, and that the police might be involved in some kind of a cover up to protect powerful people potentially implicated. Rumours also began swirling about Hiny's family receiving death threats, and the suspect allegedly boasting about being well-connected.

Beyond the whispers however, there has been precious little to substantiate the idea that stringing up Frank Akpan alone would not represent any kind of justice for Hiny Umoren. Sources willing to speak up and provide information about this case have generally not been forthcoming.

Until now.

Game Changing Information

Every telephone conversation made via a GSM telephone line has a permanent record with the mobile service provider, which by law cannot be tampered with or erased. The information captured can vary, but it always includes the following elements: the date and time the interaction was initiated; the type of interaction (voice or SMS); the length of the interaction; the number initiating the interaction; the number receiving the interaction and the location of the closest cell towers to both parties.

Some networks also record the actual conversation (voice note), and depending on the type of signal band and mobile device, it is even possible to capture the exact location of both parties, accurate to within a few metres. Anyone who can get their hands on the call data from Frank Akpan's line would very quickly be able to establish whether he was in fact acting alone – which is where my source came in handy.

Understandably, this information is meant to be impossible to access without law enforcement authorisation. With this in mind, I have taken the extra precaution of reproducing it manually via a spreadsheet, so as to protect my source by removing all possible identifying information. Over the course of several hours last week, I pored over several days' worth of leaked call data from Frank Akpan's mobile provider to make sense of the situation.

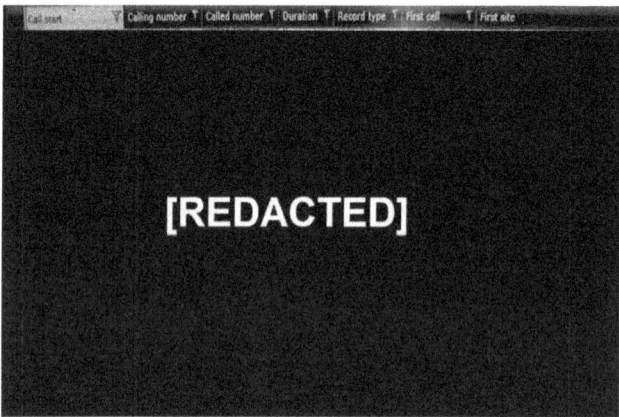

What will be presented in this story is the closest thing that exists to objective evidence that:

1.) Frank Akpan is being used to take the fall for much bigger fish involved in Hiny Umoren's murder; and

2.) While Frank Akpan is certainly the primary suspect and was directly involved in the murder, there are other participants in the murder still walking free, while the Akwa Ibom Police Command intentionally bungles what should be an open and shut investigation.

Who is Frank Akpan?

Apart from a few tidbits pieced together from social media accounts about him, very little is known about Frank Akpan the primary suspect. The timeline to his arrest begins late in the afternoon on April 29, when Umoh puts out Hiny's number hoping someone will be able to track down her friend's location.

NEFERTITI @ETUKMMA · Apr 29
Please drop her number so it can be tracked.

♡ 2   ↻ 16   ♡ 115   ↑

Happiness Activist #justiceforHinyUmoren
@UmohUduak1

Replying to @ETUKMMA and @HinyHumoren

+2348081295920

5:53 PM · Apr 29, 2021 · Twitter for iPhone

42 Retweets   **5** Quote Tweets   **173** Likes

The mention of "Frank Akpan" as a central figure in this story begins with this tweet from Umoh which identifies the owner of the Airtel number +2348127530092 as the person who invited Hiny for the supposed interview.

🍃**ZibeN** @iamziben · Apr 29

Can we get the number of who invited her for the interview? Anything please? Just the number!

💬 3   🔁 25   ♡ 179   ⬆️

Happiness Activist #justiceforHinyUmoren
@UmohUduak1

Replying to @iamziben and @HinyHumoren

+234 812 753 0092

6:57 PM · Apr 29, 2021 · Twitter for iPhone

45 Retweets **3** Quote Tweets **256** Likes

A quick check with Truecaller brings up the name "Ezekiel Akpan." Curiously, the occupation tag on this person's Truecaller profile reads "Political." It is important to bear in mind that Truecaller fills an individual's 'name' and 'occupation' fields by pulling high quality data from several sources including Facebook profile information and analysis of the individual's Facebook friend networks – so this tiny detail will become significant later on.

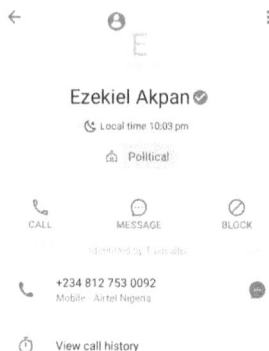

Shortly after finding himself under instant national scrutiny following Umoh's tweet, Akpan then attempts to throw the public off the scent with the Facebook post below. In so doing, he inadvertently confirms that the telephone number in question is actually his, thereby proving that "Uduak Frank Akpan" and "Ezekiel Akpan" are the same person.

Posts

🖼 Photos

Uduak Frank Akpan   •••
47 m · 🌐

Good afternoon All.
Please kindly forwarded this message to anybody that knows her, I was contacting her yesterday to her concerning a job opportunity, as at the time she called me she was at ibiaku junction, the call went off so I called back several times. After several efforts, I couldn't reach her. Below here is her name and phone number, Iniubong Umoren 08081295920. This is also her cousins name gotten from Facebook, Godsluv Udoikop. Please help me pass this message to find her or her family members. Please I am not holding her hostage nor do I know her anything about her whereabouts. My phone has been off because I've been getting threatening messages due to the misunderstanding.

Shortly thereafter, he deactivates his Facebook profile and seemingly goes silent until the Akwa Ibom State Police Command issues a statement 3 days later, confirming his arrest and effectively pronouncing him guilty of the crime as a sole suspect.

Frank Uduak Ezekiel Akpan

So far, based on the version of the story that is in official circulation, there is only Frank Akpan and the unfortunate Hiny Umoren. The police have declared him a serial rapist – and hence a single actor. Officially, the issue is over and there is nothing more to see here. It was just a horrible monster and a woman who unfortunately fell victim under the most heartbreaking circumstances.

The only counter-story so far boils down to a few unsubstantiated social media rumours that cannot stand in court, plus what would otherwise be compelling evidence from Akpan's crime scene, which unfortunately has now been contaminated and rendered all but useless for the purpose of a criminal investigation.

Bassey Ibiatisuho
@realbassey101

So today work took me to the compound where Iniubong Umoren was allegedly murdered in Nung Ikono Obio in Uruan. I saw 12 shallow graves, countless number of school books bearing different names, dresses and shoes belonging to girls, bones and filthy bags.
#JusticeForHinyUmoren

12:46 PM · May 7, 2021 · Twitter Web App

By deliberate malfeasance or by incompetence, the Akwa Ibom State Police Command has allowed key evidence from Akpan's hideout potentially pointing to a larger conspiracy, to be trampled underfoot by hundreds of curious onlookers and social media content creators. In so doing, the evidence to build a case for anything other than a standalone Frank Akpan conviction has been destroyed or rendered inadmissible.

There is however, one type of evidence that cannot be physically destroyed or tampered with in any way. This evidence has a permanent digital record which sits in cloud storage away from the incompetence or malfeasance of the Nigeria Police Force, and what it shows without a shadow of doubt is that Frank Akpan did not act alone.

Leaked Network Records: The Smoking Gun
To properly understand and contextualise the data that you are about to see below, a little explaination is in order. As mentioned earlier, the 6 categories of telephone interaction data always recorded by service providers are call date and time, originating number, receiving number, type of interaction (call or SMS), length of interaction (in seconds) and the originating/receiving cell tower.

Every cell tower on earth has a unique location code written in this format: MCC (Mobile Country Code)-MNC (Mobile Network Code)-LAC (Location Area Code)-CellID. Nigeria's mobile country code is 621, and its 4 largest network providers MTN, Glo, Airtel and 9Mobile have the respective MNCs 30, 50, 20 and 60. Using this information alongside the LAC and CellID provided in the call records below, you can pinpoint the exact cell tower closest to where the call in question was made or received.

For example, if the given MCC is 621, the MNC is 20 (Airtel), the LAC is 00784, and the CellID is 20565, you can put this information into free public access cell site locators like cell2gps.com and the result will be a cell tower site in Uyo at the junction of Ikot-Ekpene road and Ikpa Road.

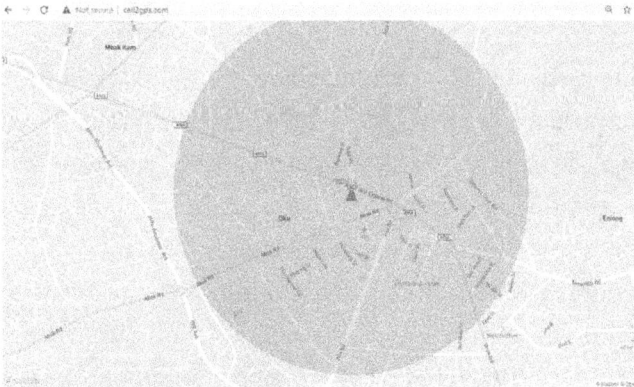

This is actual cell site data from a call made by Frank Akpan at 6.50PM on April 29, 2021

That being said, it is time to examine the leaked call record data and draw our conclusions. First, here is data

I extracted from what my source provided, showing the significant parts of Frank Akpan's call and SMS history on the day Hiny Umoren was murdered.

Call Info	Originating Number	Receiving Number	Length	Call Type	Receiving Call Tower Address	Exact Location
29/4/2021 13:09:17	08127530092 (Frank Akpan)	0906881##25 (Nonso Irohukwu Oitali)	37	Call	30-20868-64267	n/a
29/4/2021 13:17:21	08127530092 (Frank Akpan)	0906129##20 (Ihiebong Umoren)	124	Call	20-00990-15713	n/a
29/4/2021 13:21:18	08127530092 (Frank Akpan)	37016081480 (Blessing Godwin)	147	Call	30-00793-10043	n/a
29/4/2021 14:59:22	08127530092 (Frank Akpan)	0708199466.2 (Unknown Person)	26	Call (phone waved)	Originating Tower Address / 20-00996-16713	n/a
29/4/2021 15:38:35	09081296920 (Ihiebong Umoren)	08127530092 (Frank Akpan)	106	Call	20-00996-15713	n/a
29/4/2021 16:16:54	08127530092 (Frank Akpan)	08122306922 (Unknown Frequent Caller)	106	Call	20-00990-16713	n/a
29/4/2021 13:58:23	08122306922 (Unknown Frequent)	08127530092 (Frank Akpan)	32	Call	20-00784-50877	n/a
29/4/2021 10:49:11	08127530092 (Frank Akpan)	08122306922 (Unknown Frequent Caller)	0	SMS	20-00990-15713	n/a
29/4/2021 13:50:49	08127530092 (Frank Akpan)	08122306922 (Unknown Frequent Caller)	0	SMS	20-00784-20666	n/a

For ease of understanding, I ran all the numbers through Truecaller and put the names in brackets next to them

Around 1.17PM on April 29, Frank Akpan placed a call to Hiny Umoren, which lasted for 124 seconds. It is fair to extrapolate that this was a call where he gave directions to her regarding where she should go for the purported interview. At 1.21PM, he then placed a call to a Blessing Godwin, which lasted 147 seconds. Was he chatting up another potential victim of the same job interview snare? It is impossible to say for now.

At 3:38PM, Hiny Umoren then placed a call to Frank Akpan lasting for 106 seconds. If you compare the cell tower data here to that of his previous phone calls, it is clear that he was already at the supposed venue waiting for her because the tower location does not change. It is safe to assume that she was calling to tell him that she had arrived for her interview. Save for a 2-second WhatsApp voice note which Hiny later managed to send to Umoh, this call was probably the last time anyone ever heard Hiny Umoren alive again.

Around 6.15PM, almost 3 hours after Hiny Umoren arrived at his lair, Frank Akpan then placed a call to an unknown number. The call records clearly show +2348127530092 – Frank Akpan's known public number – making repeated contact between 6.15PM and 6.50PM with +2348122386922, an unknown number which brings up no details on Truecaller or Facebook. For reference, if a mobile number pulls up no Truecaller, Facebook or social media results whatsoever, this could either mean that it is used on a non-internet-enabled feature phone (a so-called 'burner' phone), or that the owner is extremely intentional about having no digital footprint linked to that number.

Incidentally, this was also around the time when the Twitter hashtag #FindHinyUmoren had already led Twitter sleuths to uncover Frank Akpan's identity, leading to his amateur attempt at misdirection referenced earlier. In the middle of a clear and obvious crisis moment, why was Frank Akpan repeatedly trying to establish contact with this unknown number with no digital footprint? The answer could lie in some data I extracted from a different set of call records showing Frank Akpan's contact with this number in the days and weeks before Hiny Umoren was murdered.

Call Info	Originating Number	Receiving Number	Length	Call Type
13/4/2021 19:43:50	08122386922 (Unknown Frequent Caller)	08127530092 (Frank Akpan)	0	SMS
13/4/2021 22:19:16	08122386922 (Unknown Frequent Caller)	08127530092 (Frank Akpan)	0	SMS
13/4/2021 19:42:57	08122386922 (Unknown Frequent Caller)	08127530092 (Frank Akpan)	0	SMS
14/4/2021 07:35:02	08122386922 (Unknown Frequent Caller)	08127530092 (Frank Akpan)	29	Call
14/4/2021 07:53:44	08122386922 (Unknown Frequent Caller)	08127530092 (Frank Akpan)	0	SMS
14/4/2021 07:23:55	08122386922 (Unknown Frequent Caller)	08127530092 (Frank Akpan)	14	Call
21/4/2021 06:21:10	08122386922 (Unknown Frequent Caller)	08127530092 (Frank Akpan)	19	Call
21/4/2021 14:07:10	08122386922 (Unknown Frequent Caller)	08127530092 (Frank Akpan)	41	Call
21/4/2021 15:31:26	08122386922 (Unknown Frequent Caller)	08127530092 (Frank Akpan)	19	Call
21/4/2021 15:33:44	08122386922 (Unknown Frequent Caller)	08127530092 (Frank Akpan)	35	Call
27/4/2021 18:53:32	08122386922 (Unknown Frequent Caller)	08127530092 (Frank Akpan)	31	Call
27/4/2021 19:31:59	08122386922 (Unknown Frequent Caller)	08127530092 (Frank Akpan)	11	Call
29/4/2021 18:28:23	08122386922 (Unknown Frequent Caller)	08127530092 (Frank Akpan)	22	Call

This unknown person contacted Frank Akpan no fewer than 12 times between April 4 and April 27

Was this a regular buyer or facilitator of whatever gruesome trade Frank Akpan was involved in? Was Frank calling him for help after an unexpected social media campaign suddenly exposed him and put their entire business operation at risk? Why was this the first number that Frank called immediately after raping and murdering a young woman? We do not know the answers to these questions, but there is at least one person other than Frank Akpan himself who can probably tell us.

The "Senior Forestry Officer"

It is April 30, 2021, and Frank Akpan has become a nationwide hate figure on social media. His involvement in Hiny Umoren's disappearance is public knowledge at this point, and time is running out for him. He needs friends and allies to protect him – and fast. His name and picture are doing the rounds on social media, and in a city like Uyo, it will not be long before someone recognises him and he finds himself subjected to Nigerian street justice.

Between 10.27Am and 10.44AM, he places 3 phone calls to a Francisca Bassey Akpan – Francisca is in Calabar when she receives the calls, and she is using a smartphone in a location with high network capacity, which means the network is able to record her location while receiving Frank's calls to within a few metres of accuracy.

Call Info	Receiving Number	Terminating Number	Length	Call Type	Receiving Cell Tower Address	Exact Location
30/4/2021 10:27:18	08127530092 (Frank Akpan)	09183884864 (Bassey Francisca Akpan)	22	Call	60-21451-13032	Opposite ABC Park, Along IBB Way, Calabar
30/4/2021 10:31:17	08127530092 (Frank Akpan)	09183884864 (Bassey Francisca Akpan)	37	Call	60-21451-13032	Opposite ABC Park, Along IBB Way, Calabar
30/4/2021 10:44:18	08127530092 (Frank Akpan)	09183884864 (Bassey Francisca Akpan)	52	Call	60-21451-15002	22, Ediba Road, Calabar Municipal, Cross River
30/4/2021 10:55:00	09183884864 (Bassey Francisca Akpan)	08127530092 (Frank Akpan)	51	Call	60-21451-11513	No.9, Edim Otop Close, Off Victory Way, Calabar
30/4/2021 16:33:53	09127530092 (Frank Akpan)	08812635320 (Kufre Effiong)	31	Call	30-13066-05642	5A, East Housing Estate, G-Line, Uyo, Akwa Ibom
30/4/2021 16:34:41	08038967819 (Kufre Effiong)	08127530092 (Frank Akpan)	226	Call	20-00097-37413	5B, East Housing Estate, G-Line, Uyo, Akwa Ibom
30/4/2021 16:38:10	08038967819 (Kufre Effiong)	08127530092 (Frank Akpan)	0	SMS	30-13066-37218	n/a
30/4/2021 16:39:13	08127530092 (Frank Akpan)	08038967819 (Kufre Effiong)	0	SMS	30-13066-27218	n/a
30/4/2021 16:39:13	08038967819 (Kufre Effiong)	08127530092 (Frank Akpan)	0	SMS	20-00097-37413	n/a
30/4/2021 16:46:12	08127530092 (Frank Akpan)	08034386056 (BP Ezeugo Samuel)	93	Call	30-13022-05646	n/a
30/4/2021 19:36:41	06182284553 ("The Police Man")	08127530092 (Frank Akpan)	2	Call	60-21462-20592	Police Station by Barrack Road, Uyo, Akwa Ibom

At 10.55AM, Francisca calls Frank back. Only they and the mobile network know what is said during this 51-second conversation. My source balked at the idea of obtaining customer voice notes because that would simply be a bridge too far, even for the sake of solving a brutal murder. Just getting this much information to me is already breaking multiple in-house rules and NCC codes, so they understandably did not want to push their luck.

At 4.32PM on April 30, Frank then makes one of the most interesting phone calls in this entire story. Truecaller pulls up the details of the recipient of the phone call with the number +23480★★★★★326 – one "Kufre Effiong." Unlike the other people Frank has been known to associate with, Kufre Effiong appears to be from a different world. He is significantly older than Frank and as his location details show, he lives in the swanky part of town. Who is this guy?

< Search   Add to contacts

Kufre Effiong ⊘
● last seen 2d ago
Add Tags

Call   Message   Voice   Flash

Identified by Truecaller

Mobile - MTN Nigeria

Their conversation lasts for just 31 seconds and presumably ends with Kufre hanging up. Frank's phone rings almost immediately at 4.34PM. The caller is +234803★★★★★19 and this conversation lasts decidedly longer than the last one – almost 4 minutes. Who is the owner of this number that has so much to talk about with someone who is probably Nigeria's most wanted man at the moment? Truecaller answers once again.

‹ Search Add to contacts

Kufre Effiong ✓

last seen 2d ago

Add Tags

| Call | Message | Voice | Flash |

Identified by Truecaller

Mobile - MTN Nigeria

Kufre Effiong is an older, wealthier looking man who apparently spends his time in the upscale Ewet Estate while Frank Akpan rapes and murders young women in uncompleted buildings somewhere across town.

What could these two possibly have in common that brings them together? Interestingly, if you compare the location data from both calls, it is clear that both men have in fact met physically at a certain 58G, Ewet Housing Estate in Uyo. Frank is probably outside the building talking to this older, wiser man on the phone and hoping to get some help from him.

More on 58G, Ewet Housing Estate later.

Who exactly is Kufre Effiong? I eventually found the answer after scrolling through dozens, maybe hundreds of social media profiles with that exact name. Mr Effiong as it turns out, is something of a big fish in Niger Delta civil service circles.

Intro

SFO at Federal Ministry of Niger Delta Affairs

Went to festac college festac town lagos nigeria

Studied at Command Secondary School Jos

Studied at University of Calabar, Nigeria

Lives in Abuja, Nigeria

From Nung Ikono Ufok, Akwa Ibom, Nigeria

Married

Posts

Filters

Kufre Effiong updated his profile picture
April 9, 2020

Beautiful days ahead...

Source: Facebook

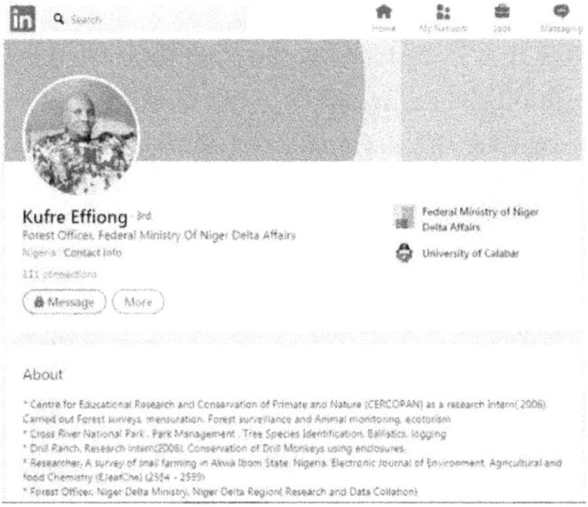

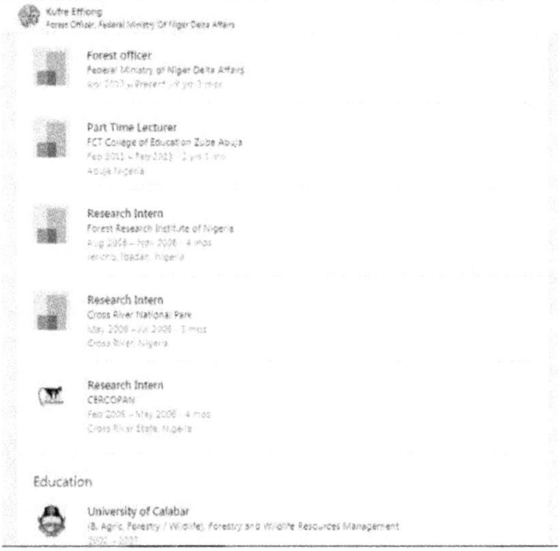

Source: LinkedIn

Now back to the address where both men met. Plot 58, G Unit, Ewet Housing Estate is home to the Uyo branch office of a medical NGO called the Center for Clinical Care and Research (CCCR Nigeria).

Founded in 2010 by an all-star list of accomplished Nigerian-American doctors, CCCR carries out medical outreach programs in underserved areas of Nigeria and promotes medical best practices using a fusion of global best practices and local healthcare delivery models. Or at least it used to, because as far as it is possible to tell, its social media pages have had no activity whatsoever since 2017. A scan of news stories since 2017 using the keywords "CCCR Nigeria" and "Center for Clinical Care and Research Nigeria" turns up nothing.

Source: Facebook

And yet, at least if Google is to be believed, its Uyo branch office at 58, G Unit, Ewet Housing Estate still opens at 8.30AM everyday and closes at 5PM. This exact address also happens to be where Kufre Effiong made and received calls from Frank Akpan, who also physically met him there 24 hours after raping and murdering Hiny Umoren.

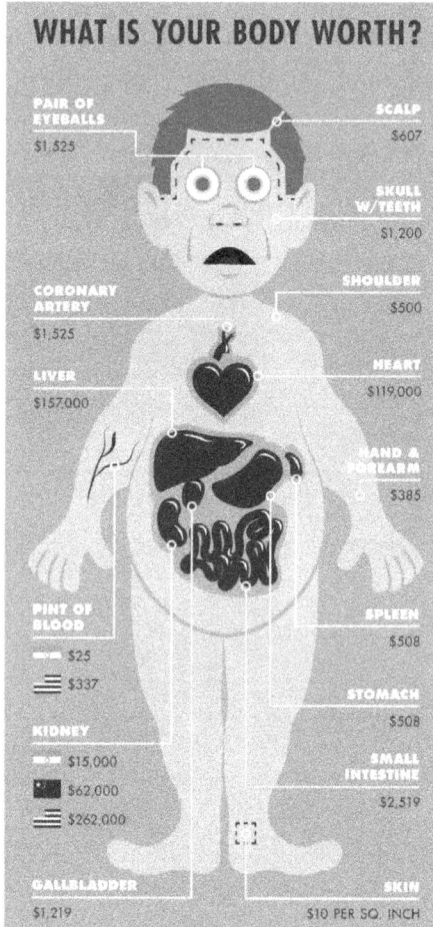

Black market value of human organs | Source: Gizmodo

Due to the convoluted house numbering system in Uyo, the property labeled as 58, G Unit, Ewet Housing Estate is also recognised on most digital maps as Plot S.9, Unit G, Ewet Housing Estate. That address is also home to Davok Suites, which is a popular upmarket hotel in Uyo favoured by high profile guests including the Cameroon national team.

Source: Hotels.com

This would be the ideal location for a trusted associate of a politician – say, a senior civil servant – to lay his head while running a clandestine errand for his boss.

An errand such as sourcing human parts for use

in a ritual sacrifice ahead of the upcoming election season, for example. Whatever it is that happened or is happening at 58, G Unit, Ewet Housing Estate – and for whose benefit – is a question only Kufre Effiong can answer. Cavernous as this story has become, there is still one more twist.

Hiny Umoren's Murder – A Police Cover up in Progress

At the outset, I referenced a press release from the Akwa Ibom State Command on May 2 patting themselves on the back for arresting Frank Akpan and solving a huge criminal conspiracy in 5 minutes by pinning everything on him. One of the names singled out for praise in the press release for his alleged role in apprehending Frank Akpan was a certain SP Samuel Ezeugo.

'On 30/04/2021, the Command received a report on the disappearance of the victim.

'Following available leads, men of the Anti-Kidnapping Squad of the Command, led by CSP Inengive Igosi, consolidated on the initial great progress made by the DPO Uruan, SP Samuel Ezeugo and arrested the perpetrator who confessed to have lured his victim to his house in the guise of giving her a job, but ended up sexually and physically assaulting her which led to her death.

'To cover his tracks, he dragged and buried her in a shallow grave in his father's compound,' Mr MacDon, a superintendent of police, said in the statement.

The body of the woman has been exhumed and deposited at the University of Uyo Teaching Hospital, Uyo, the police said.

'Suspect is a confessed serial rapist who has owned up to the raping of other victims.

On April 30, at 4.40PM, Frank Akpan placed a call to someone with the number +2348034386086.

Call Info	Receiving Number	Terminating Number	Length	Call Type	Receiving Cell Tower Address	Exact Location
30/4/2021 10:27:16	08127530092 (Frank Akpan)	08163884864 (Bassey Francisca Akpan)	22	Call	60-21451-13032	Opposite ABC Park, Along IBB Way, Calabar
30/4/2021 10:31:17	08127530092 (Frank Akpan)	08163884864 (Bassey Francisca Akpan)	3F	Call	60-21451-13032	Opposite ABC Park, Along IBB Way, Calabar
30/4/2021 10:44:18	08127530092 (Frank Akpan)	08163884864 (Bassey Francisca Akpan)	62	Call	60-21451-15802	22, Edika Road, Calabar Municipal, Cross River
30/4/2021 10:55:06	08163884864 (Bassey Francisca Akpan)	08127530092 (Frank Akpan)	51	Call	60-21451-19613	No 9, Efem Otop Close, Off Victory Way, Calabar
30/4/2021 16:33:63	08127530092 (Frank Akpan)	09032719926 (Kufre Effiong)	31	Call	30-13093-05642	58, Ewet Housing Estate, G-Line, Uyo, Akwa Ibom
30/4/2021 16:34:41	09036907819 (Kufre Effiong)	08127530092 (Frank Akpan)	225	Call	30-00997-37411	58, Ewet Housing Estate, G-Line, Uyo, Akwa Ibom
30/4/2021 16:39:10	09036907819 (Kufre Effiong)	08127530092 (Frank Akpan)	0	SMS	30-13093-27218	n/a
30/4/2021 16:39:13	08127530092 (Frank Akpan)	09036907819 (Kufre Effiong)	0	SMS	30-13093-27218	n/a
30/4/2021 16:35:13	09036907819 (Kufre Effiong)	08127530092 (Frank Akpan)	0	SMS	20-00997-37413	n/a
30/4/2021 16:46:12	08127530092 (Frank Akpan)	08034394088 (9P Ezeugo Samuel)	93	Call	30-13022-05146	n/a
30/4/2021 19:38:41	08192254620 ("The Police Man")	08127530092 (Frank Akpan)	2	Call	60-21462-20992	Police Station by Barrack Road, Uyo, Akwa Ibom

Second from bottom

At this point, I trust it will not shock you to know that when I ran this number through Truecaller, the name that came up was none other than...

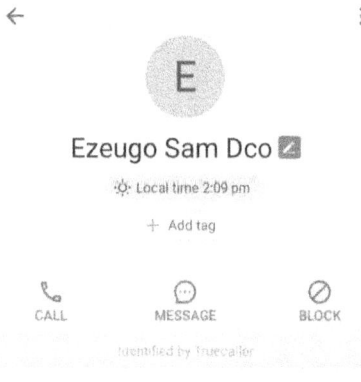

←   ⋮

E

Ezeugo Sam Dco

☀ Local time 2:09 pm

+ Add tag

📞   ☺   ⊘
CALL   MESSAGE   BLOCK

Identified by Truecaller

The one and the same.

In other words, while the Akwa Ibom Police Command is releasing statements claiming to be solving a crime by arresting a suspect, the suspect was actually making telephone calls to one of the police officers who would later "arrest" him, and speaking to him for a minute and a half. What were they talking about?

Perhaps Frank Akpan – who was still at large at the time – was giving SP Ezeugo instructions for how to apprehend him nicely?

Even more conveniently, Akpan placed the call to SP Ezeugo less than a minute after receiving a text message from Kufre Effiong. While still physically located at 58, G Unit, Ewet Housing Estate.

In other words, the senior civil servant working at the Niger Delta Ministry probably sent SP Ezeugo's phone number to Akpan via SMS, with instructions to call him and let him "handle" it.

And most tellingly of all, SP Ezeugo's cell tower location data indicates that while all this was happening, he was in close range of a cell tower near the entrance of Ewet Housing Estate. Presumably, on his way to meet oga.

Take note of the cell tower's location next to General Edet Akpan Avenue

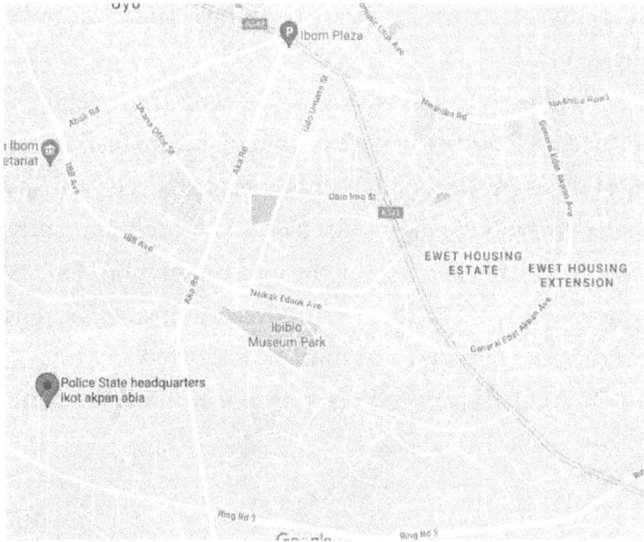

For comparison, look at Ewet Housing Estate vis-a-vis General Edet Akpan Avenue

So putting the entire picture together, we have what appears to be a well-connected criminal gang in Akwa Ibom with links to the police and the Federal Ministry of the Niger Delta, which probably specialises in sourcing human organs either for the purpose of selling to the international black market or to service local politicians who believe in ritual human sacrifice.

By the accident of targeting someone with significant social media capital, the existence of this organisation is threatened, and so the Akwa Ibom Police Command is allegedly being used to actively bungle and mishandle the case.

Finding the individual who owns the telephone number +2348★★★★★★★22 is central to unraveling the mystery of why Iniobong Umoren had to die, how many more like her have died in the past, and most importantly, who are the big fish behind the entire operation. Exactly what is going on at 58, G Unit, Ewet Housing Estate is another key question that must be answered.

If Frank Akpan won't talk, maybe Kufre Effiong can tell us.

XI

AIR PEACE AND A STORY ABOUT POOR NIGERIAN REGULATION

Nigeria's busiest airline appears to have declared war on a customer - with connivance from the authorities. Why is this happening?

Christopher Ogbonna is not a firebrand revolutionary.

This becomes abundantly clear after speaking with him a couple of times. He is a soft-spoken lawyer who dotes on his wife and talks with a sizeable dose of dad humour. Harmless as he comes across, these are strange times for him. For the best part of 2 years now, he has lived like a cat, slipping quietly in and out of Nigeria and keeping his location secret at all times. In this line of work, I have dealt with sources who have taken several types of precautions when passing information across to me before, but nothing comes close to his level of paranoia.

There have been sources who sent information anonymously via Dropbox. There have been sources who communicated exclusively using self-destructing messages on Signal and Telegram. There was once a source who heard an echo during an encrypted voice conversation and concluded I was recording, which led to the abrupt end of that lead despite my repeated denial of the accusation. There was even a source who only agreed to speak to me provided I could show up in person to a quiet warehouse at Silicon Oasis in Dubai to receive a handwritten note.

Christopher however, is the first source ever to pass documents across using what turns into a complex dead drop involving a flash drive and multiple intermediaries who do not know each other or what the package they are ferrying contains. Using this convoluted method, Christopher's pen drive finds its way to my [redacted location] abode, where I finally get my hands on it. My 2 Windows PCs have been targeted **by Nigerian government-sponsored malware attacks before and may be compromised, so I plug the pen drive into my non-networked Linux PC and hope for the best.**

What shows up on the screen is a treasure trove of documents that tell a story about how Nigeria's busiest commercial airline seemingly has no scruples about telling lies, falsifying records and flagrantly flouting rules in an attempt to score a Pyrrhic victory against its own customer. For almost 2 years, the story of one man's struggle against this powerful airline owned by a well-connected billionaire entrepreneur has been consigned to the fringes of mainstream coverage. Now for the first time, West Africa Weekly can tell the story of Air Peace and its headscratching mission to squash Christopher and his wife Nneka.

He Said, They Said...

The story starts on December 19, 2019, when Nneka Ogbonna boards Air Peace flight 7210 from Murtala Mohammed International Airport in Lagos to Osubi airstrip in Warri, Delta State. At the door of the aircraft, she is accosted by an air hostess who informs her that her carry-on luggage will have to be checked in. Anyone who is a regular Nigerian Twitter user has likely seen the following account of what happened next, written by her husband Christopher.

For those who have not seen it already, a cliff notes version:

- Nneka insists that her carry-on can fit in the overhead locker and that she has traveled with it several times before.
- The air hostess insists that Nneka must check the bag in and at this point, the Captain of the

flight, Horace Miller-Jaja steps in and angrily demands that she should do as she is told, which she does.

- Captain Miller-Jaja does not stop there however, but continues to shout angry invective and insults at her using the plane's PS system, despite the fact that she is seated with her seatbelt on at this point.

- FAAN officials soon arrive and ask her to leave the plane because Captain Miller-Jaja has said that he will not fly if she is on the flight.

- Nneka refuses to leave her seat which she has paid for, and Captain Miller-Jaja turns off the plane's engine and cooling system in the late morning heat, effectively using physical and psychological torture against his passengers so they can put pressure on her to deboard.

- She is eventually forced off the plane by FAAN and CAA officials who physically manhandle her out of her seat. One male official even places his hands in between her buttocks while this is happening.

- Once she is bundled off the plane, the doors are closed and the flight takes off without her. She is forced to write a statement about what happened and handed over to the police, who then seize her international passport.

- When Chris later writes a Twitter thread detailing what happened, Air Peace then responds with a very different account of events.

RESPONSE TO CHRISTOPHER OGBONNA'S POST

Mrs. Nneka Ogbonna (the passenger) checked in for a flight from Lagos to Warri on December 10, 2019. She arrived at the foot of the aircraft with a luggage for boarding but the reasons she was deboarded have grossly been misrepresented.

She was informed by our boarding staff that she would not be able to have the bag as a carry-on luggage. The staff explained to her that the aircraft was a 50-seater Embraer Jet, which is smaller than a Boeing, and that the other passengers had utilised most of the space in the overhead cabin.

The staff requested that the bag be tagged and checked-in. Mrs Ogbonna refused to submit her bag as requested. Rather she pushed past the staff and made her way into the aircraft.

Inside the aircraft, she was again advised by the air hostess that because of the aircraft's limited capacity for carry-on items, she should release her bag for storage in the cargo hold. She refused, stating that since the bag was already tagged as a carry-on, it must not be checked in.

Our staff explained to her that carry-on bags are allowed subject to availability of space and safety. She was also reminded that safety was paramount for us and that it would be unsafe to carry her luggage in her preferred way.

Mrs. Ogbonna blatantly refused to bulge. All this time, she positioned herself at the entrance of the aircraft making it impossible for other passengers to continue boarding. It took the intervention of some passengers before she eventually released the bag to be checked-in about thirty minutes later.

This was after throwing a tirade at the flight crew. She thereafter continued to make videos of those in the aircraft and hurled more insults at our staff.

When her unruly attitude became intolerable, the Pilot-in-Command asked that she be deboarded.

She refused and stood on the stairs of the aircraft. Even when the airport security was invited, she was unyielding.

This prompted a call for reinforcement from FAAN. It was however not until the pilot shut down the engine of the aircraft at 12:15pm that she was successfully disembarked. We then referred the matter to the Airport Police Command.

It is important to state that the pilot had approached Mrs. Ogbonna to inquire what the matter was and returned to his seat when she threw insults at him. His act was in exercise of his pre-flight requirement as commander of the aircraft as required by the Civil Aviation Regulations. There was no time that the pilot acted contrary to the Regulations.

We are shocked at Mr Christopher's rendering of the incident. At no time was Mrs Ogbonna harassed, intimidated, or assaulted, whether sexually or otherwise. In fact, the airport security was invited to ensure due process was followed.

.

The passenger's unruly conduct was a threat to peace hence a report was made to the Police whose responsibility it is to maintain peace and order. We cannot speak for the modalities employed by the Police in their investigation as they are an independent body.

It is an affront to allude that there was an attempt by any of our staff to extort Mrs. Ogbonna. We were notified of the intention of the passenger to settle out of court by the Police and a letter from the law firm of Partners Associates & Co. During the meeting, we stated our terms, which basically consisted of the loss suffered because of the delay occasioned by Mrs. Ogbonna's actions

Rather than attempt to meet us, at least, half-way, the passenger and her solicitor insisted that they were not going to fulfil any of the terms. The Police intervened and rescheduled the meeting. The passenger refused to honour the invitation as well as subsequent invitations.

We opine that Mrs. Ogbonna is looking for means to avoid the consequence of her action as well as frustrate the investigations of the police. This attitude should not be encouraged.

We refuse to be intimidated by the demands in the letter from her solicitor as our actions in this matter have been with due regard for the laws of our country. We also categorically deny Mrs. Ogbonna's claim that her passport is being held by the Police on our instruction.

Clearly both accounts cannot be true at the same time, so what actually happened on that day? In developing this story, I have delved not only into the facts of the public battle between Air Peace and the Ogbonna family, but the disturbing reality of important Nigerian regulatory institutions that actively avoid doing their job and place certain individuals and entities literally above the law. It is a story about corporate dishonesty, legal skulduggery, individual shamelessness, regulatory malfeasance, disappearing data and forged documents - the exact things that have traditionally led to disasters in Nigeria's aviation sector.

Horace the Screaming Pilot vs Nneka the Pretty "Hijacker"

Captain Horace Miller-Jaja is a recently retired passenger pilot whose profile looks as prosaic as it is competent. Having spent the best part of 3 decades flying commercially, he recently took charge of his final flight on May 5, 2021. Looking at the few public recordings that exist of him, he is exactly what you would picture an experienced pilot to look like - grey haired, soft spoken and with an apparently calm and gentle demeanour.

When our story begins on December 10, 2019 however, Captain Miller-Jaja is presumably not having a good day. Exactly why this is the case nobody really knows, but what he is about to do will reveal more about

Nigeria's aviation sector than any number of official reports and press statements can. He is standing at the door of the cockpit ahead of a Lagos-Warri flight, and he does not take kindly at all to the sight of a woman arguing about her carry-on luggage with the air hostess. That woman is Nneka Ogbonna.

A legal deposition from the ongoing court case describes what happens next:

27. At this point, the 1st Plaintiff noticed that the 5th Defendant who was standing at the entrance of the aircraft, was scowling at her. Suddenly, the 5th Defendant interrupted the conversation between the 1st Plaintiff and the 1st Defendant's air hostess in a most unprofessional, rude and uncivil manner, and asked the 1st Plaintiff if she was **_stupid or deaf_**? It was such an unwarranted and unprovoked outburst from someone so responsible and elderly-looking that the 1st Plaintiff was temporarily shocked and stunned. The 5th Defendant then shouted at her again in a very abrasive and threatening manner, and rudely ordered her to immediately comply with the air hostess' instructions or she would not be allowed to fly with the aircraft.

28. The 1st Plaintiff was surprised and embarrassed by the 5th Defendant's unprovoked outburst, so she told him calmly that she did not appreciate either his use of abusive language or being humiliated publicly. Her response visibly angered the 5th Defendant and he further raised his voice to intimidate the 1st Plaintiff.

29. To avoid further embarrassment from the 5th Defendant, the 1st Plaintiff fully complied with the punitive order of the 5th Defendant by leaving the entrance of the aircraft and descending the stairway to the base of the aircraft where she surrendered her hand luggage. Her hand luggage was tagged and placed in the aircraft's cargo hold before she climbed up again to board the aircraft. _The Plaintiffs plead and shall rely on the 1st Defendant's baggage tag which was subsequently issued to her at the base of the aircraft which appears on page 14 of the Plaintiffs' Bundle of Documents._

Apparently, Captain Miller-Jaja is having a really bad day indeed, because even after being incredibly rude to this passenger, he comes back for more. At this point, when the issue has seemingly been solved and the matter should be over, he launches a verbal tirade at Nneka Ogbonna and keeps on doing so even after she has taken her seat and fastened her seatbelt. The deposition continues:

31. Having complied fully with the 5th Defendant's punitive instructions and surrendered her hand luggage which had previously been approved as cabin baggage for tagging and placement in the cargo hold, the 1st Plaintiff expected to be left in peace to board the aircraft and settle down in her seat before take-off.

32. However, the 5th Defendant was not yet satisfied with his humiliation, harassment, intimidation and bullying of the 1st Plaintiff. He continued to utter unprovoked invectives at the 1st Plaintiff even as she made for her seat. The 1st Plaintiff was embarrassed by the 5th Defendant's conduct and requested that he stopped abusing her. She further told him that save for the fact that she was respecting him as an older adult, she would have responded in like manner to him. After that, the 1st Plaintiff ignored the 5th Defendant, located her seat, sat down and fastened her seatbelt.

33. Shortly after the 1st Plaintiff sat down on her seat and fastened her seat belt, employees of the 1st Defendant approached the 1st Plaintiff while she was seated on her seat with her seatbelt fastened and requested her to leave the aircraft.

For reference, the "1st plaintiff" in the deposition is Nneka Ogbonna; the "1st Defendant" is Air Peace; and the "5th Defendant" is Captain Horace Miller-Jaja. Nneka is now seated at her assigned Seat 4A with her seatbelt fastened, and there should no longer be an issue, but it is now apparent that Captain Miller-Jaja must be having the worst day ever, because he completely loses all control and composure after Nneka's rebuke mentioned in the above deposition.

Where the plane's passengers are probably used to hearing aircraft PA systems carrying the soothing, slightly boring voice of level-headed, unruffled pilots, something unfolds that most of them have probably never seen before. 63 year-old Captain Miller-Jaja grabs the cockpit PA system and begins to yell insults into it, screaming at Nneka to leave the plane and inciting other passengers to force her off the aircraft if they want him to fly them to their destination.

For good measure, Captain Miller-Jaja then turns off the plane's engines and air conditioning system in the late morning heat of the Lagos airport tarmac for maximum discomfort to all of his passengers.

Air Peace staff then approach Mrs Ogbonna and inform her that the Captain has ordered her off the plane. They go on to erroneously inform her that Captain Miller-Jaja can decide at will to fly or not to fly anyone as he pleases, and that if she does not leave the plane, she will be charged with a criminal offense.

Air Peace station manager Isa Aminu Suleman further attempts to gaslight Mrs Ogbonna by claiming that she must leave the aircraft because she has brought an overweight bag into the aircraft. She points out that the bag in question is no longer on the aircraft and has been sent for check-in, and Suleman realises that he has no leg to stand on. Staff of the Nigeria Civil Aviation Authority (NCAA) and the Federal Airports Authority of Nigeria (FAAN) get involved at the request of Captain Miller-Jaja and the deposition describes what happened next.

56. Subsequently, on the instructions of the 5ᵗʰ Defendant, a female employee of the 3ʳᵈ and 4ᵗʰ Defendants approached the 1ˢᵗ Plaintiff from the front, loosened her seatbelt, grabbed her by her belt and started dragging her out with so much force that the belt was damaged. When the belt was cut, her pair of jeans trousers which she was wearing loosened and her inner clothing became exposed. *The Plaintiffs plead and shall rely on the damaged belt a picture of which appears on page 42 of the Plaintiffs' Bundle of Documents as well as proof of the cost of replacing the damaged belt which appears on page 43 of the Plaintiffs' Bundle of Documents.*

57. Then, two male employees of the 3ʳᵈ and 4ᵗʰ Defendants (one wore an Aviation Security (AVSEC) identity card with number 25870 bearing the name "Fatoyinbo" and the other who introduced himself as Nze, Head of Crime and Investigation) stood behind the 1ˢᵗ Plaintiff, grabbed her by her trousers and underwear and inserted their hands into her buttocks and attempted to strip her naked while dragging her away from her seat.

58. **Isa Aminu Suleman** (the 1ˢᵗ Defendant's Station Manager) recorded the entire sordid incident on a mobile device from a vantage point which clearly captured Nze and Fatoyinbo in the sordid acts of battering, assaulting and sexually assaulting the 1ˢᵗ Plaintiff. Isa Aminu Suleiman can also be heard in the 1ˢᵗ Plaintiff's video recording encouraging Nze and Fatoyinbo to use **_"maximum force"_** on the 1ˢᵗ Plaintiff and that the 5ᵗʰ Defendant had instructed them to use **_"maximum force"_** to remove the 1ˢᵗ Plaintiff from the aircraft.

Air Peace Counterattacks

The full and unredacted account of what happened next is impossible to reproduce here. Suffice to say that it contains intrigue and skulduggery far too voluminous and sometimes mundane to possibly fit into this newsletter. For brevity sake, here is an abridged version of how it goes:

- Nneka Ogbonna is forcefully bundled out of her seat and off the flight with so much force that her clothing belt is severed, causing her jeans to fall and her underwear to become exposed.
- NCAA and FAAN staff hand her over to the police and she is forced to write a criminal suspect statement after being accused of "hijacking" the plane by Captain Miller-Jaja.
- Air Peace staffers convince the police to seize Nneka Ogbonna's international passport.
- When Nneka eventually gets back to Warri and reunites with her husband, they hire a lawyer who writes to the management of Air Peace requesting a settlement meeting. A presumed understanding is reached and the meeting is fixed for January 9, 2020 at the DPO's office of the Domestic Air Division, Ikeja, Lagos.
- They show up at the meeting only to discover that it is a ruse by Air Peace to bully them and extort money from them. Air Peace lawyers Deborah Bazuaye and Adedoyin Adeniji present a demand notice for N3,070,000, allegedly as "compensation for making the flight take off late."

- The police proceed to hold on to Nneka's passport for a further 8 months until they eventually return it to the immense chagrin of Air Peace.

- The Ogbonnas write to the NCAA and FAAN. The NCAA responds with a letter that reads like a middle finger to them. The letter refuses to acknowledge their concerns and it infers that Captain Miller-Jaja is not subject to any oversight. It also denies that the clearly-identified NCAA staff wearing a name tag who was involved in the incident is actually employed by the NCAA and even suggests that the agency should not be joined in the lawsuit.

NIGERIAN CIVIL AVIATION AUTHORITY

P.M.B. 21029, 21038, IKEJA-LAGOS.

NCAA

NCAA/DG/AIR/11/16/135

22nd June, 2020

Mrs. Nneka Ogbonna

Dear Madam,

RE: NOTICE OF INTENTION TO COMMENCE SUIT: RE MRS. NNEKA OGBONNA AND 6 ORS WITH NCAA (3RD DEFENDANT)

We hereby acknowledge receipt of your notice to commence suit as captioned above and dated 27th May, 2020.

The Nigerian Civil Aviation Authority (NCAA) to be sued as the 3rd Defendant in the intended suit is the regulatory body of aviation in Nigeria.

The NCAA carries out oversight functions which includes ensuring the safety of aircraft, persons and properly carried in aircraft and preventing aircraft from endangering persons and property in accordance with the provisions of the Civil Aviation Act 2006 and also in line with the provisions of the Civil Aviation Regulations.

The NCAA has never shirked in its responsibilities of ensuring the safety and security of air passengers and their baggage.

You may wish to note the following provisions of S. 45 (1) (2) (3) of the Civil Aviation Act 2006 which provides for the security check of persons and baggage of every person entering the aerodrome and boarding an aircraft which could be done by any person authorized by the Authority.

You may also note that it is the responsibility of the Pilot in Command to ensure the safety of all passengers including checking and reacting appropriately to ensure the safety and the operational efficiency of the flight before take-off.

We have noted your averments in paragraphs 5,6,7,8,25,26,34,39,41,43,44,45, and 58 of your statement of claim and the reliefs sought by you in paragraphs 10,11, 12, 13, 20,21,22, 23 and 24 of your claims and declarations.

In response to all of your claims and declarations as listed above, we wish to state as follows:

1.   That the Nigerian Civil Aviation Authority (NCAA) (3rd Defendant) does not have any

Corporate Headquarters : Nnamdi Azikwe Int'l Airport, Domestic Wing, Abuja.
Tel :+234 (1) 7610041, +234 (1) 7610042, +234 (1) 7610043 , +234 (1) 7610044, **Tel/Fax** : +234 807 729 1113,
Lagos Office: AVIATION HOUSE, Murtala Mohammed International Airport (MMIA) Domestic Wing, Ikeja.
Tel: +234 (1) 4721521 **Fax:** +234 (1) 2790421 **Consumer Protection:** +234 (1) 7607286 (24hrs); **Airworthiness:** +234 (1) 4734482;
Licencing: +234 (1) 7739972; **Operations:** +234 (1) 4714339; **Switch Board:** +234 (1) 7610036, +234 (1) 7610037.
Email: info@ncaa.gov.ng Website:www.ncaa.gov.ng

body known as "Fatoyinbo" in the Consumer Protection Directorate or Aviation Security Department.

2.   That the NCAA does not use or wear "Name Tags" as a means of identification of its personnel or employees.

In view of the above we wish to state that we are wrongly joined in this intended suit.

You may therefore wish to reconsider your stand on your intention to join the 3rd defendant.

Thanking you for your cooperation

Emmanuel Dubem Chukwuma
Emmanuel Dubem Chukwuma
Legal Adviser/Head, Compliance and Enforcement
For: Director-General.

When Christopher Ogbonna uploads video evidence of Captain Miller-Jaja's unprofessional behaviour and his wife's mistreatment on his social media pages, Air Peace deletes its version **of the story from its social media handles. As the true details of the case start to make their way into the court process and Air Peace stares at an impending humiliating loss of face, the airline changes tack and turns to legal dark arts to frustrate the Ogbonnas out of seeking justice. Company lawyers file a fresh accusation against Nneka Ogbonna, alleging that she carried a "dangerous or explosive substance" into the aircraft.**

31. That the Applicant when seated in the aircraft, in utter defiance to the hardship she had put the 1ˢᵗ Respondent, its staff and other flying passengers through, brought out her phone and put a call across to her supposed husband despite instructions from the cabin crew that mobile phones and electronic gadgets are to be switched off or not allowed to be used on board the aircraft.

32. That after spending about 30 minutes with her supposed husband, Mr. Christopher Ogbonna who actively encouraged her to disobey the cabin

crew and the 5ᵗʰ Respondent who is the commander of the Plane on phone against instructions, as her mobile phone was on speaker mode so that everyone could hear her conversation with him, she became more unruly than ever and boasted openly that her husband instructed her not to obey the cabin crew instruction and she remained adamant and her attitude got every other passengers on board the plane talking.

33. That I know as a fact that the 5ᵗʰ Respondent warned her that her actions is criminal and tantamount to taking the plane hostage as the drama lasted for close to one hour and continued the waste of aviation fuel, as the Plane engine was running preparatory to take off.

34. That the Applicant was never forcefully disembarked from the plane rather the AirPeace security reported the crime of holding the plane to ransom by the Applicant to the Airport Divisional Police who in the exercise of their investigative powers invited the Applicant. That Applicant clearly stated in her audio that "Honey Achorom Igbada: meaning in English "Honey I want to get down"

35. That I am informed by J.K. Mbanefo Ikwegbue Esq., of counsel on 5ᵗʰ October, 2020 in a meeting in their office at Plot 767 Idris Gidado Street, (Beside Roses Regency Hotel), Wuye District, Abuja by 12:00 noon and I verily believe him that the action of the applicant contravenes the **Criminal Law of Lagos State 2011, Section 240 (D)** and this Section carries the punishment of life imprisonment.

36. That in addition to Paragraph 38 hereof, I am informed by J.K. Mbanefo Ikwegbue Esq., of counsel on 5ᵗʰ October, 2020 in a meeting in their office at Plot 767 Idris Gidado Street, (Beside Roses Regency Hotel), Wuye District, Abuja by 12:00 noon and I verily believe him that the narratives of the applicant as found in paragraph 21(x) amounts to a breach of peace in a public place which is also a crime.

37. That the Applicant indeed deliberately flouted this criminal law and has ran to this Honourable Court to seek protection from criminal prosecution.

38. That I know as a fact that **Nigerian Police Force** by virtue of **Section 4 of Police Act** is empowered to investigate crime and as such have done no more than invite the Applicant to explain her own side of the allegation complained against her.

39. That I also know as a fact that the action of the Applicant herein is an infraction to the criminal provisions of the **Nigerian Civil Aviation Act Section 17 97.1**.

▲ lagosministryofjustice.org

Offences Endangering Life or Health

239. Incapacitating in order to commit felony or misdemeanour

Any person who with intent to commit or facilitate the commission of a felony or a misdemeanour, uses any means calculated to choke, suffocate, strangle, stupefy or in order to incapacitate another person, commits a felony and is liable on conviction to imprisonment for life.

240. Act intended to cause serious harm or prevent arrest

Any person who, with intent to do grievous harm to any person in order to resist or prevent the lawful arrest or detention of any person—

(a) unlawfully wounds or does any grievous harm to any person by any means whatsoever;

(b) unlawfully attempts in any manner to strike any person with any kind of projectile or with a spear, sword, knife, or other dangerous or offensive weapon;

(c) unlawfully causes any explosive substance to explode;

(d) sends or delivers any explosive substance or other dangerous or noxious thing to any person;

[Volume 1]

Facing legal bullying and threats in this David vs Goliath situation, Christopher and Nneka flee to the USA, while Christopher continues pursuing justice through the Nigerian legal system. The case remains in court to date as Air Peace inexplicably digs its heels in defending the most bizarre of lost causes.

The Curious Case of the Disappearing Booking

Like most airlines, Air Peace uses an Airline Reservation System (ARS) which simplifies the process of managing seat inventory and allocating it to passengers. When a customer goes to the Air Peace website and makes a paid booking, the ARS automatically generates a unique booking reference code that is permanently tied to their booking.

When a customer enters this booking reference and their surname on the "Manage My Booking" tab on the website homepage, the ARS instantly pulls up all information related to that booking including the flight itinerary, check-in status, seat number and so on. For example, in August 2020 I bought an Air Peace Lagos-Asaba return ticket with the booking reference ALPMHF.

When I hit "OK," the following details come up:

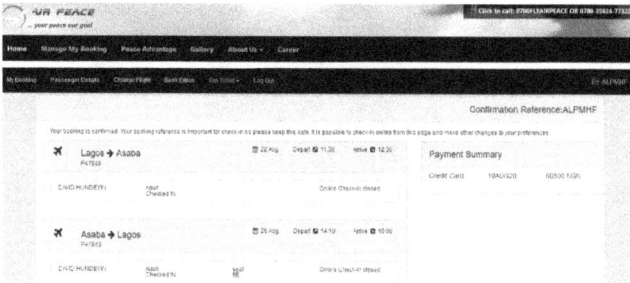

Now at this point, it is established fact that Nneka Ogbonna bought an Air Peace Lagos-Warri one-way ticket for December 10, 2019. For good measure, I even got my hands on her GT Bank debit alert email, her electronic and physical boarding passes, and her hand luggage tags.

M Gmail   Christopher Ogbonna <christopher.c.ogbonna@gmail.com>

Fwd: Boarding Pass
2 messages

Nneka Ogbonna <houseofnitd@gmail.com>   Sun, May 17, 2020 at 11:29 AM
To: Christopher Ogbonna <christopher.c.ogbonna@gmail.com>

--------- Forwarded message ---------
From: <no-reply@flyairpeace.com>
Date: Tue, Dec 10, 2019 at 7:16 AM
Subject: Boarding Pass
To: <HOUSEOFNITD@gmail.com>

 **AIR PEACE**
... your peace our goal

Boarding pass

MRS NNEKA OGBONNA

Flight number	Date	Departure time
P47210	10DEC2019	11:00
Seat number	From	Boarding
	Lagos	10:40
4A	To	
	Warri	Booking reference
	SEQ:5 TKT:710 2305200955/1	AKGK5P
Gate		
-}-		
Fold		

 **AIR PEACE**
... your peace our goal

Boarding pass

MRS NNEKA OGBONNA

Flight number	Date	Departure time
P47210	10DEC2019	11:00
Seat number	From	Boarding
	Lagos	10:40
4A	To	
	Warri	Booking reference
	SEQ:5 TKT:710 2305200955/1	AKGK5P
Gate		
-}-		
Fold		

https://mail.google.com/mail/u/0?ik=8c20175588&view=pt&search=all&permthid=thread-f%3A1689273180896165592&simpl=msg-f%3A1689933... 1/2

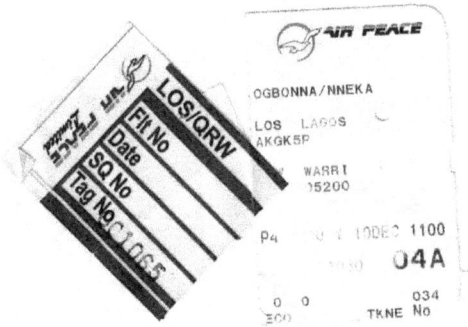

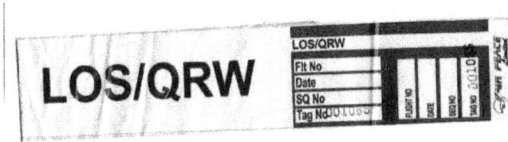

So we know without a shadow of doubt that Nneka bought a ticket, showed up for her flight, checked in successfully, got her boarding pass and boarded the aircraft before Captain Miller-Jaja had his meltdown. Her booking reference was AKGK5P. Sometime last year, Christopher happened to put her booking reference into the Air Peace ARS and this was what came up.

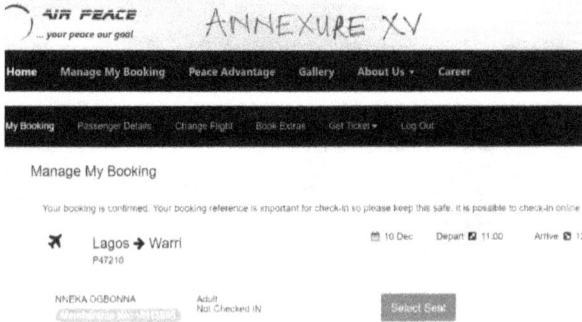

The implication of this brazen piece of data tampering by Air Peace is that the flight which Nneka boarded on December 10, 2019 supposedly does not have her on the passenger manifest. The clearly checked-in passenger is suddenly marked as "Not Checked In." This screenshot is among the documents Christopher gets across to me, and I decide to see for myself what comes up when I put her booking details into the Air Peace ARS. So that is exactly what I do - and this is what I see:

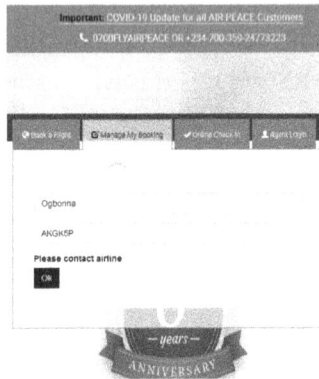

Instead of taking me to her (already fraudulently edited) booking reference page, Air Peace has now apparently decided that Nneka Ogbonna's booking never existed in the first place. The record showing that she bought a ticket for that flight has been scrubbed from the company's ARS back end. As far as Air Peace is concerned, reality is now whatever it wants it to be.

REALITY CAN BE WHATEVER I WANT IT TO BE

Even more concerning is the revelation that to date, Air Peace has not submitted the recording from the Cockpit Voice Recorder (CVR) to the relevant authorities. This would easily be the most accurate way of establishing what actually happened on December 10, 2019. If indeed Nneka Ogbonna is a terrorist hijacker who somehow boarded an Air Peace flight with an explosive or dangerous item without a valid ticket; and Captain Horace Miller-Jaja was heroically protecting the other passengers from Nneka the Terrorist, the data from the CVR should clear all doubts.

Unfortunately, the letter below provides an unpleasant clue as to what the fate of that recording might have been.

NIGERIAN CIVIL AVIATION AUTHORITY

NCAA

P.M.B. 21029, 21038, IKEJA-LAGOS.

ALL OPERATORS LETTER (FSG 003)

Ref:	NCAA/FSG/AOL/19/003
Date:	30th July, 2019
To:	All Aircraft Operators
From:	Nigerian Civil Aviation Authority
Attn:	Director of Flight Operations/Chief Pilot/Safety Manager

Subject: CONTINUOUS OVERWRITING OF COCKPIT VOICE RECORDER (CVR) INFORMATION

The purpose of this FSG All Operators Letter (AOL) is to alert all aircraft operators on the continuous overwriting of Cockpit Voice Recorder (CVR) information by their flight crew members and the necessity to ensure compliance with the appropriate Nigeria Civil Aviation Regulations (Nig. CARs) requirements.

Background

The Nigerian Civil Aviation Authority (NCAA) has noticed that airline operators' flight crew members are in the practice of continuously overwriting the CVR information. This practice makes it impossible for the Accident Investigation Bureau (AIB) to retrieve actual data to aid in its investigation as required by Paragraphs 25 and 26 of the Civil Aviation (Investigation of Air Accidents and Incidents) Regulations 2019. This action has also impeded and posed undesirable difficulty in ensuring that AIB successfully discharge its statutory mandate of investigating accidents and serious incidents

Nig. CARs Part 7.8.1.3 (b), which is derived from the provisions of ICAO Annex 6, Section 11.6 states that, "To preserve flight recorder records, flight recorders shall be deactivated upon completion of flight time following an accident or incident. The flight recorders shall not be reactivated before their disposition as determined in accordance with the accident/incident regulations of Nigeria".

Furthermore, Nig. CARs Part 8.14.10.3 (a) requires that "The operator/owner of the aircraft, or in the case where it is leased, the lessee, shall ensure, to the extent possible, in the event the aircraft becomes involved in an accident or incident, the preservation of all related flight recorder records and, if necessary, the associated flight recorders, and their retention in safe custody pending their disposition as determined by the Accident Investigation Bureau.

The operational requirement of the flight recorders by the flight crew as detailed in Nig. CARs, Part 8.5.1.24 (b) and (c) require that "The PIC may not permit a flight data recorder or cockpit voice recorder to be disabled, switched off or erased during flight, unless necessary to preserve the data for an accident or incident investigation" and "in event of an accident or incident, the PIC shall act to preserve the recorded data for subsequent investigation upon completion of flight" respectively.

The content of this letter is meant for the addressee only. If you receive this letter by error of circulation, please do not hesitate to return it to the NCAA
Corporate Headquarters: Nnamdi Azikiwe Int'l Airport, Domestic Wing, Abuja.
Tel: +234 (1) 7610041, +234 (1) 7610043, Fax: 234 807 725 1313
Lagos Office: AVIATION HOUSE, Murtala Mohammed International Airport (MMIA) Domestic Wing, Ikeja
Tel: +234 (1) 2790499; Tel/Fax: +234 (1) 2790421, Consumer Protection: +234 (1) 7607286 (24hrs);
Airworthiness: Tel: +234 709 104 4630; Fax: +234 (1) 7610044; Licencing: +234 (1) 7739672; Operations: +234 (1) 7614071
Switch Board: +234 (1) 7610036, +234 (1) 7610037; Email: info@ncaa.gov.ng; Website: www.ncaa.gov.ng

---

Actions Required:

All operators of aircraft with CVR installed are hereby required to:

1. Conduct in-house awareness training for their flight crews on the requirements of Nig. CARs Parts 7.8.1.3 (b), 8.14.10.3 (a) and 8.5.1.24 (b) and (c) immediately on receipt of this AOL.

2. Develop/Emphasize appropriate procedures addressing the requirements of Nig. CARs Parts 7.8.1.3 (b), 8.14.10.3 (a) and 8.5.1.24 (b) and (c) and incorporate same in their respective Operations Manual. This amendment must be submitted to the Authority for review, acceptance and approval within thirty (30) days from the date of issue of this AOL. These procedures must form part of the contents of the Indoctrination training for flight crew members; and

3. Ensure continuous compliance with the requirements of the Nig. CARs on the preservation of flight recorder records.

The Authority will apply its enforcement processes, where non-compliances to the requirements of the Nig. CARs or non-conformance to the operator's approved procedures have been noticed.

Please, comply accordingly.

Capt. A.M. Sidi
Director, Operations and Training
For: Director General.

In other words, it is common practice for Nigerian airlines to illegally overwrite CVR recordings, which makes it all but impossible to establish the facts of incidents like that of December 10, 2019. Has Air Peace overwritten the CVR data from that day and hidden crucial evidence? It is impossible to say, and the company has not responded to my questions at press time. However based on the foregoing, it is hard not to conclude that there is certainly precedent for this kind of behaviour at Nigeria's busiest commercial airline.

It also bears mentioning that Air Peace founder Allen Onyema has an indictment in the US District Attorney's Office for the Northern District of Georgia.

The indictment, which is for money laundering and bank fraud, contains several recurring charges of concealment of information and forgery of key documents.

Air Peace is clearly no stranger to playing fast and loose with facts, truth and documentation. According to the US District Attorney's Office, its founder and CEO shares similar values. Even worse, regulators within the aviation sector such as the NCAA appear to think that their job is to "play ball" with powerful airlines instead of regulating them. Under NCAA regulations for example, the penalty for intentional falsehoods and alterations of records such as those outlined in this story is revocation of its operating license. Guess who that will never happen to.

B 865

Violation	Recommended Sanction per Violation	Certificate Action
(h) Failure to monitor and record enroute radio communications.	Moderate to maximum civil penalty.	
(i) Deliberate violation—intentional false or fraudulent entry ; reproduction, or alteration in record or report.		Revocation.
(j) Deliberate violation—other.		180 day suspension to revocation.
11. Operation of an unairworthy Aircraft.		
(a) Technical non-conformity to type certificate, but no likely effect (potential or actual) on safe operation.	Minimum civil penalty.	
(b) Non-conformity which may have, or has, an adverse effect on safety of operation.	Moderate to maximum civil penalty.	
(c) Release of aircraft without required equipment.	Moderate to maximum civil penalty.	Up to 7 day suspension.
12. Provisions specific to passenger-carrying.		

If this airline's ability to get away with major infractions looks surprising, a little peek behind the curtain might explain why. In May 2019, the airline appointed **7 new directors, some of whom are among the most influential people in Nigeria. Among the directors are Mutiu Sunmonu, former MD of Shell Petroleum Development Company (SPDC) Nigeria, and current Chairman of Julius Berger PLC.**

Also included is Chief Nnaemeka Ngige (SAN), one of Nigeria's most influential lawyers and a public figure whose recent birthday celebration elicited official congratulatory statements from Attorney General Abubakar Malami, Secretary General to the Federation Boss Mustapha, and President Muhammdu Buhari. Present in person at the celebration were Ondo State governor Rotimi Akeredolu, former Anambra Governor

Peter Obi, and current Nigerian Bar Association president Olumide Akpata.

Also on the list of Air Peace directors is a certain Engr. Benedict Adeyileka, who so happens to be the current Rector of the International Aviation College (IAC), Ilorin, and former Director General of the NCAA - the very agency that supposedly regulates Air Peace.

Against this backdrop, it is no surprise that consumer protection regulators such as the Federal Competition and Consumer Protection Commission

(FCCPC) and its chair Tunde Irukera have no interest in picking fights with Air Peace. While the facts of the furious persecution of the Ogbonnas and concealment of evidence by Air Peace have been in the public domain for nearly 2 years, the exchange below is an example of this regulator engaging in insincere shadow-boxing and refusing to engage robustly.

In other words, the referees on the field of play in the Nigerian aviation space are wearing the colours of one of the competing teams under their refereeing shirts. As far as Nigerian regulation is concerned, Air Peace and its CEO are quite literally above the law. They can mistreat and physically assault customers, hide and destroy evidence illegally, modify and delete data fraudulently, engage in legal gymnastics to frustrate consumers, and carry out offenses that should ordinarily lose them their operating license - and no such thing will ever happen.

This is an exceedingly dangerous situation for Nigerian air travelers, and here is why.

Deleted Records, Screaming Pilots and Dodgy Maintenance - All Symptoms of the Same Disease
On May 22, 2010, Air India Express flight 812 from Dubai to Mangalore crashed on landing and killed 158 of 166 people onboard. The reason for the crash? Despite 3 calls from the 1st Officer to "Go Around" (abort landing and reattempt), Captain Zlatko Glušica

made the decision to land despite having overshot the touchdown point by several hundred metres.

He then worsened the error by attempting to abort the landing after touching down. The plane overshot the runway, fell into a ravine and burst into flames. The subsequent accident investigation revealed that Captain Glušica had slept **for over 90 minutes during the flight, and he was likely to be cognitively impaired, or not operating with optimal judgment during the landing. The CVR in fact recorded him snoring loudly in the cockpit.**

In a field like aviation, human error due to bad judgment or cognitive impairment has a very high chance of leading to fatal outcomes. The good news is that despite a number of safety incidents and near-misses over the years including burst tires **and** collapsed nose wheels **during landing, Air Peace to its credit, has never registered a fatal accident. The bad news is that it only takes one incident for that record to be wiped. Just one.**

One maintenance engineer who might be willing to tick a box saying that something has been done when it hasn't been done.

One corrupt or compromised regulator who will give an approval that should not be given because Air Peace is too powerful to be regulated.

One ill tempered pilot who reacts to the mild stressor that is a passenger carry-on bag dispute with the screaming tantrums of a 63 year-old man-child.

It only takes one. In 2012, it took one pilot making the decision to press on to Lagos on one engine instead of landing at the nearest possible airfield. Dana Air Flight 992 became one of the worst aviation disasters in Nigeria's history, and I personally lost a friend and schoolmate, Kunbi Adebiyi.

Between the incredibly defective internal company culture at Air Peace which I have covered **before, and the regulators looking the other way as this airline repeatedly breaks the law and acts with impunity, the conditions for another huge Nigerian aviation disaster are mounting.**

The signs are already here.

ACKNOWLEDGMENTS

I wish to thank the following people who have been instrumental in different ways and at different points in my personal and professional life:

Mercy Abang, who gave me my first major break in investigative reporting;

Fola Folayan, without whom a lot of the work that went into this book could simply not have happened;

Prof Onyeka Nwelue, who needs no introduction;

Adebayo Raphael, my brother in the #EndSARS struggle and fellow Nigerian-in-exile;

Ndi Kato, whose key contributions to my personal and professional growth are difficult to overstate;

Tayo Fagbule, who somehow found a way to keep publishing my BusinessDay column despite the problems that came with being publicly associated with me in Nigeria;

Ojie Imoloame, who for 15 years has been a trusted friend and a valuable resource person;

Rinu Oduala, my "coconut head" little sister in whom I am well pleased;

My cousins Sade, David, Dami, Seyon, Laotan, Sesi, Isaac, Debbie, Pedetin, Olumide and my aunt Mrs Modupe Coker.

From the bottom of my heart, I thank you all for being there for me.

ABOUT THE AUTHOR

Over most of the course of an award-laden 10-years in Journalism, David Hundeyin has dedicated himself to telling Nigeria's most forbidden stories in a uniquely ferocious voice that has earned him a huge following and a long list of powerful enemies. This 1-man mission to peel back decades of necrosis in Nigerian journalism has made him contemporary Nigeria's most recognisable journalist as well as one of its most controversial personalities.

He is the Distinguished James Currey Fellow at the Centre of African Studies in the University of Cambridge.

www.ingramcontent.com/pod-product-compliance
Lightning Source LLC
Chambersburg PA
CBHW020534030426
42337CB00013B/850